War and Morality

Basic Problems in Philosophy Series

A. I. Melden and Stanley Munsat

General Editors

Human Rights
A. I. Melden

Morality and the Law
Richard A. Wasserstrom

War and Morality
Richard A. Wasserstrom

The Analytic-Synthetic Distinction
Stanley Munsat

Civil Disobedience and Violence
Jeffrie G. Murphy

Guilt and Shame
Herbert Morris

Wadsworth Publishing Company, Inc.
Belmont, California

War and Morality

Edited by
Richard A. Wasserstrom
University of California, Los Angeles

Wadsworth Publishing Company, Inc.   Belmont, California

ISBN 0-534-79950-7

L. C. Cat. Card No.: 75-117742

Printed in the United States
of America

4 5 6 7 8 9 10—74 73 72 71

Series Foreword

The Basic Problems in Philosophy Series is designed to meet the need of students and teachers of philosophy, mainly but not exclusively at the undergraduate level, for collections of essays devoted to some fairly specific philosophical problems.

In recent years there have been numerous paperback collections on a variety of philosophical areas and topics. Those teachers who wish to refer their students to a set of essays on a specific philosophical problem have usually been frustrated, however, since most of these collections range over a wide set of issues and problems. The present series attempts to remedy this situation by presenting together, within each volume, key writings on a single philosophical issue.

Given the magnitude of the literature, there can be no thought of completeness. Rather, the materials included are those that, in the judgment of the editor, must be mastered first by the student who wishes to acquaint himself with relevant issues and their ramifications. Thus, historical as well as contemporary writings are included.

Each volume in the series contains an introduction by the editor to set the stage for the arguments contained in the essays and also a bibliography to help the student who wishes to pursue the topic at a more advanced level.

A. I. Melden
S. Munsat

Richard Alan Wasserstrom is a professor of law
and a professor of philosophy at the University of
California, Los Angeles. He received a B.A. degree
from Amherst College, an M.A. and a Ph.D. from the
University of Michigan, and an LL.B. from Stanford
University. As well as teaching at Stanford and
U.C.L.A., he has served as an attorney in the Civil
Rights Division of the Justice Department and as
Dean of the College of Arts and Sciences at
Tuskegee Institute. He has published a book,
The Judicial Decision (1961), and several articles,
including "The Obligation to Obey the Law," *U.C.L.A.
Law Review*, Vol. 10 (1963).

Contents

Introduction   1

The Moral Equivalent of War, William James   4

The Morality of Obliteration Bombing, John C. Ford, S. J.   15

War and Murder, Elizabeth Anscombe   42

Moral Judgment in Time of War, Michael Walzer   54

Pacifism: A Philosophical Analysis, Jan Narveson   63

On the Morality of War: A Preliminary Inquiry, Richard
    Wasserstrom   78

Judgment and Opinion, The International Tribunal,
    Nuremberg, Germany   102

Superior Orders, Nuclear Warfare, and the Dictates of
    Conscience, Guenter Lewy   115

Selected Bibliography   135

Introduction

Philosophers of the Western world have worried, by and large, comparatively little about the subject of war. As a result, the philosophical literature that is devoted to this topic is less rich and less adequate than that which focuses upon any number of other, somewhat analogous subjects. Much more philosophical energy has, for example, been devoted to the general subject of law than to that of war.

Similarly, the more specific topic of this collection, the morality of war, has also been neglected. In part, this neglect is no doubt due to a reluctance in contemporary analytic philosophy to deal with problems of normative ethics rather than topics of a metaethical character. But this cannot be the whole answer because it does not explain either the relative neglect of the topic in recent non-analytic philosophy or the comparable avoidance in the philosophical undertakings of the past. Nor, for that matter, does this explanation even consider the fact that topics such as the morality of civil disobedience and the appropriateness of legally enforcing sexual morality have, quite recently, received substantial attention from analytic philosophers.

As the readings that follow indicate, the group most concerned with problems of the morality of war has been the philosopher-theologians; and within this group the Catholic philosophers, beginning perhaps with Augustine, have historically shown the greatest interest and sophistication. It is at least worth considering—as a kind of secondary question—what there is about the tradition of Catholic philosophy that has made this issue seem genuine and important. Similarly, it is also worth asking whether there is something about the whole topic of war that might make philo-sophical inquiry appear to be especially difficult or unproductive.

The fact that the general subject of war has been bypassed by philosophers has certain consequences for any adequate considera-tion of the problem, and more particularly, for the readings contained in this collection. For there are, to put it simply, a variety of issues that have been inadequately sorted out and a number of problems that have been insufficiently attended to. I want to mention only two that seem to me to stand out as essential but that are not adequately addressed in any of the readings that follow.

The first problem is the most typical of all philosophical considerations: the definition or nature of war. People talk a good deal about war, but what do we really mean when we say of something that it is a war? To what degree, for instance, is the notion of the involvement of nation-states caught up in the very meaning of *war*? Can there be wars if countries are not involved? Or, to take a related question, how are wars to be distinguished from a variety of other phenomena with which they might be confused? Is there a difference between a war and a revolution? Between a war and an insurrection? Between a war and a rebellion? Between an act of war and an act of piracy? Nor does this exhaust the definitional problems. Does the kind or magnitude of force used determine whether something is a war? Can there meaningfully be rules of war? Laws of war? The list of questions can surely be extended appreciably. The point is, however, that the analysis of the concept of war has received insufficient attention in philosophical literature and, as a result, in these readings.

The second essential area relates to the variety of concerns that can be embraced within a discussion of the morality of war. Just consider, for example, the discussions that can take place both in everyday life and in philosophy. Someone will maintain that all war is immoral; another that it is immoral or unjust for a country to be fighting a particular war; still a third that there is nothing wrong with war provided it is not a war of aggression. Assertions such as these are common, but they are too ambiguous to be dealt with sensibly. They are in fact composed of, or dependent upon, a number of more specific claims that must be identified before genuinely informed discussion and analysis can proceed.

There are, in particular, at least three sets of questions that deserve to be distinguished in discussions of the morality of war. The first relates to the behavior of countries as opposed to persons. When persons talk about the morality of war, they sometimes appear to be assessing the intentions and behavior of persons and sometimes the intentions and conduct of countries. But are countries assessable on moral grounds in the same way and for the same reasons that persons are? The second area concerns the rightness or wrongness of an action when contrasted with the praise or blame resulting from that behavior. Someone can do the wrong thing and nonetheless be free of blame. When persons talk about the morality of war, what are the relevant categories—those of rightness-wrongness, those of praiseworthiness-blameworthiness, or both? The third area involves the differences between particular acts, particular wars, and war as an institution. It is one thing to evaluate the morality of individual actions leading up to or taking place within a war; another thing to evaluate the morality of a particular war; and still a third to assess the morality of war as a human phenomenon. Although the symmetry is perhaps imperfect, the differences seem no less significant than those between an individual law, a particular legal system, and the idea of a legal system. Yet discriminations of this order are seldom made even in the philosophical literature.

Still more subtle discriminations are both possible and appropriate, though even less often noted. Consider, for example, the different things that might count as individual actions in respect to war: (1) the action of an individual person occurring at a particular time and place (for instance, an ordinary foot soldier shooting and killing an unarmed prisoner, although not ordered to do so); (2) the action of an individual person in ordering others to do something (for instance, a battalion commander orders his men to shoot and kill all of the prisoners they have taken); (3) the action of a group of persons acting collectively (for instance, a bomber squadron dropping incendiary bombs in a particular raid on a particular city); and (4) various kinds of continuing actions by persons or groups (such as commanding or fighting a particular campaign).

Equally complicated is the question of how the evaluation of an institution differs from the evaluation of its constituents. For example, to take the case of law again, it is crucial to identify the relevant criteria for deciding whether a particular law is just or unjust, or moral or immoral, and to determine if these differ at all from the criteria for deciding whether a particular legal system is just or unjust, or moral or immoral. Then there is the further question of whether either or both of these differ from the relevant criteria (if there are any) for deciding whether all legal systems are and must be unjust or immoral. And analogous problems in respect to war surely exist and deserve attention.

Other questions altogether, or more refined versions of these questions, will doubtless occur to each reader as he confronts the following selections from recent writings on the morality of war. This collection will, in my judgment, not be a distinctive success if it answers for anyone most of the important questions concerning the morality of war. But the collection will be a success, and a significant one at that, if it convinces people that fundamental questions do in fact exist—questions upon which the peculiar abilities of philosophy can most appropriately and importantly be brought to bear.

William James
The Moral Equivalent
of War

4   The war against war is going to be no holiday excursion or camping party. The military feelings are too deeply grounded to abdicate their place among our ideals until better substitutes are offered than the glory and shame that come to nations as well as to individuals from the ups and downs of politics and the vicissitudes of trade. There is something highly paradoxical in the modern man's relation to war. Ask all our millions, north and south, whether they would vote now (were such a thing possible) to have our war for the Union expunged from history, and the record of a peaceful transition to the present time substituted for that of its marches and battles, and probably hardly a handful of eccentrics would say yes. Those ancestors, those efforts, those memories and legends, are the most ideal part of what we now own together, a sacred spiritual possession worth more than all the blood poured out. Yet ask those same people whether they would be willing in cold blood to start another civil war now to gain another similar possession, and not one man or woman would vote for the proposition. In modern eyes, precious though wars may be, they must not be waged solely for the sake of the ideal harvest. Only when forced upon one, only when an enemy's injustice leaves us no alternative, is a war now thought permissible.

It was not thus in ancient times. The earlier men were hunting men, and to hunt a neighboring tribe, kill the males, loot the village and possess the females, was the most profitable, as well as the most exciting, way of living. Thus were the more martial tribes selected, and in chiefs and peoples a pure pugnacity and love of glory came to mingle with the more fundamental appetite for plunder.

William James was for many years a professor of philosophy at Harvard. He resigned his professorship in 1907 at the age of sixty-five and died three years later. He wrote and lectured widely on a variety of topics in or related to philosophy. Among his more well-known writings are *Principles of Psychology* (1890), *The Varieties of Religious Experience* (1902), *Pragmatism* (1907), and *A Pluralistic Universe* (1909).

This essay, "The Moral Equivalent of War," was published in leaflet form in 1910 by the Association for International Conciliation. More than 30,000 copies of the leaflet were distributed, and the essay also appeared in several popular magazines. It also was published in *Memoirs and Studies* (1911), pp. 265-297. Reprinted with the permission of Alexander R. James, Literary Executor.

Modern war is so expensive that we feel trade to be a better avenue to plunder; but modern man inherits all the innate pugnacity and all the love of glory of his ancestors. Showing war's irrationality and horror is of no effect upon him. The horrors make the fascination. War is the *strong* life; it is life *in extremis*; war-taxes are the only ones men never hesitate to pay, as the budgets of all nations show us.

History is a bath of blood. The *Iliad* is one long recital of how Diomedes and Ajax, Sarpedon and Hector *killed*. No detail of the wounds they made is spared us, and the Greek mind fed upon the story. Greek history is a panorama of jingoism and imperialism—war for war's sake, all the citizens being warriors. It is horrible reading, because of the irrationality of it all—save for the purpose of making "history"—and the history is that of the utter ruin of a civilization in intellectual respects perhaps the highest the earth has ever seen.

Those wars were purely piratical. Pride, gold, women, slaves, excitement, were their only motives. In the Peloponnesian war, for example, the Athenians ask the inhabitants of Melos (the island where the "Venus of Milo" was found), hitherto neutral, to own their lordship. The envoys meet, and hold a debate which Thucydides gives in full, and which, for sweet reasonableness of form, would have satisfied Matthew Arnold. "The powerful exact what they can," said the Athenians, "and the weak grant what they must." When the Meleans say that sooner than be slaves they will appeal to the gods, the Athenians reply: "Of the gods we believe and of men we know that, by a law of their nature, wherever they can rule they will. This law was not made by us, and we are not the first to have acted upon it; we did but inherit it, and we know that you and all mankind, if you were as strong as we are, would do as we do. So much for the gods; we have told you why we expect to stand as high in their good opinion as you." Well, the Meleans still refused, and their town was taken. "The Athenians," Thucydides quietly says, "thereupon put to death all who were of military age and made slaves of the women and children. They then colonized the island, sending thither five hundred settlers of their own."

Alexander's career was piracy pure and simple, nothing but an orgy of power and plunder, made romantic by the character of the hero. There was no rational principle in it, and the moment he died his generals and governors attacked one another. The cruelty of those times is incredible. When Rome finally conquered Greece, Paulus Aemilius was told by the Roman Senate to reward his soldiers for their toil by "giving" them the old kingdom of Epirus. They sacked seventy cities and carried off a hundred and fifty thousand inhabitants as slaves. How many they killed I know not; but in Etolia they killed all the senators, five hundred and fifty in number. Brutus was "the noblest Roman of them all," but to reanimate his soldiers on the eve of Philippi he similarly promises to give them the cities of Sparta and Thessalonica to ravage, if they win the fight.

Such was the gory nurse that trained societies to cohesiveness. We inherit the warlike type; and for most of the capacities of heroism that the human race is full of we have to thank this cruel history. Dead men tell no tales, and if there were any tribes of other type than this they have left no survivors. Our ancestors have bred pugnacity into our bone and marrow, and thousands of years of peace won't breed it out of us. The popular imagination fairly fattens on the thought of wars. Let public opinion once reach a certain fighting pitch, and no ruler can withstand it. In the Boer War both governments began with bluff but couldn't stay there, the military tension was too much for them. In 1898 our people had read the word "war" in letters three inches high for three months in every newspaper. The pliant politician McKinley was swept away by their eagerness, and our squalid war with Spain became a necessity.

At the present day, civilized opinion is a curious mental mixture. The military instincts and ideals are as strong as ever, but are confronted by reflective criticisms which sorely curb their ancient freedom. Innumerable writers are showing up the bestial side of military service. Pure loot and mastery seem no longer morally avowable motives, and pretexts must be found for attributing them solely to the enemy. England and we, our army and navy authorities repeat without ceasing, arm solely for "peace," Germany and Japan it is who are bent on loot and glory. "Peace" in military mouths today is a synonym for "war expected." The word has become a pure provocative, and no government wishing peace sincerely should allow it ever to be printed in a newspaper. Every up-to-date dictionary should say that "peace" and "war" mean the same thing, now *in posse*, now *in actu*. It may even reasonably be said that the intensely sharp competitive *preparation* for war by the nations *is the real war*, permanent, unceasing; and that the battles are only a sort of public verification of the mastery gained during the "peace" interval.

It is plain that on this subject civilized man has developed a sort of double personality. If we take European nations, no legitimate interest of any one of them would seem to justify the tremendous destructions which a war to compass it would necessarily entail. It would seem as though common sense and reason ought to find a way to reach agreement in every conflict of honest interests. I myself think it our bounden duty to believe in such international rationality as possible. But, as things stand, I see how desperately hard it is to bring the peace-party and the war-party together, and I believe that the difficulty is due to certain deficiencies in the program of pacificism which set the militarist imagination strongly, and to a certain extent justifiably, against it. In the whole discussion both sides are on imaginative and sentimental ground. It is but one utopia against another, and everything one says must be abstract and hypothetical. Subject to this criticism and caution, I will try to characterize in abstract strokes the opposite imaginative forces, and point out what to my own very fallible mind seems the best utopian hypothesis, the most promising line of conciliation.

In my remarks, pacificist though I am, I will refuse to speak of the bestial side of the war-*regime* (already done justice to by many writers) and consider only the higher aspects of militaristic senti- ment. Patriotism no one thinks discreditable; nor does any one deny that war is the romance of history. But inordinate ambitions are the soul of every patriotism, and the possibility of violent death the soul of all romance. The military patriotic and romantic-minded every- where, and especially the professional military class, refuse to admit for a moment that war may be a transitory phenomenon in social evolution. The notion of a sheep's paradise like that revolts, they say, our higher imagination. Where then would be the steeps of life? If war had ever stopped, we should have to re-invent it, on this view, to redeem life from flat degeneration.

Reflective apologists for war at the present day all take it religiously. It is a sort of sacrament. Its profits are to the vanquished as well as to the victor; and quite apart from any question of profit, it is an absolute good, we are told, for it is human nature at its highest dynamic. Its "horrors" are a cheap price to pay for rescue from the only alternative supposed, of a world of clerks and teachers, of co-education and zo-ophily, of "consumer's leagues" and "associated charities," of industrialism unlimited, and feminism unabashed. No scorn, no hardness, no valor any more! Fie upon such a cattleyard of a planet!

So far as the central essence of this feeling goes, no healthy minded person, it seems to me, can help to some degree partaking of it. Militarism is the great preserver of our ideals of hardihood, and human life with no use for hardihood would be contemptible. Without risks or prizes for the darer, history would be insipid indeed; and there is a type of military character which every one feels that the race should never cease to breed, for every one is sensitive to its superiority. The duty is incumbent on mankind, of keeping military characters in stock—of keeping them, if not for use, then as ends in themselves and as pure pieces of perfection,—so that Roosevelt's weaklings and mollycoddles may not end by making everything else disappear from the face of nature.

This natural sort of feeling forms, I think, the innermost soul of army-writings. Without any exception known to me, militarist authors take a highly mystical view of their subject, and regard war as a biological or sociological necessity, uncontrolled by ordinary psychological checks and motives. When the time of developmet is ripe the war must come, reason or no reason, for the justifications pleaded are invariably fictitious. War is, in short, a permanent human obligation. General Homer Lea, in his recent book "The Valor of Ignorance," plants himself squarely on this ground. Readiness for war is for him the essence of nationality, and ability in it the supreme measure of the health of nations.

Nations, General Lea says, are never stationary—they must necessarily expand or shrink, according to their vitality or decrepitude. Japan now is culminating; and by the fatal law in question it is impossible that her statesmen should not long since have entered, with extraordinary foresight, upon a vast policy of conquest—the game in which the first moves were her wars with China and Russia and her treaty with England, and of which the final objective is the capture of the Philippines, the Hawaiian Islands, Alaska, and the whole of our Coast west of the Sierra Passes. This will give Japan what her ineluctable vocation as a state absolutely forces her to claim, the possession of the entire Pacific Ocean; and to oppose these deep designs we Americans have, according to our author, nothing but our conceit, our ignorance, our commercialism, our corruption, and our feminism. General Lea makes a minute technical comparison of the military strength which we at present could oppose to the strength of Japan, and concludes that the islands, Alaska, Oregon, and Southern California, would fall almost without resistance, that San Francisco must surrender in a fortnight to a Japanese investment, that in three or four months the war would be over, and our republic, unable to regain what it had heedlessly neglected to protect sufficiently, would then "disintegrate," until perhaps some Caesar should arise to weld us again into a nation.

A dismal forecast indeed! Yet not unplausible, if the mentality of Japan's statesmen be of the Caesarian type of which history shows so many examples, and which is all that General Lea seems able to imagine. But there is no reason to think that women can no longer be the mothers of Napoleonic or Alexandrian characters; and if these come in Japan and find their opportunity, just such surprises as "The Valor of Ignorance" paints may lurk in ambush for us. Ignorant as we still are of the innermost recesses of Japanese mentality, we may be foolhardy to disregard such possibilities.

Other militarists are more complex and more moral in their considerations. The "Philosophie des Krieges," by S. R. Steinmetz is a good example. War, according to this author, is an ordeal instituted by God, who weighs the nations in its balance. It is the essential form of the State, and the only function in which peoples can employ all their powers at once and convergently. No victory is possible save as the resultant of a totality of virtues, no defeat for which some vice or weakness is not responsible. Fidelity, cohesiveness, tenacity, heroism, conscience, education, inventiveness, economy, wealth, physical health and vigor—there isn't a moral or intellectual point of superiority that doesn't tell, when God holds his assizes and hurls the peoples upon one another. *Die Weltgeschichte ist das Weltgericht;** and Dr. Steinmetz does not believe that in the long run chance and luck play any part in apportioning the issues.

The virtues that prevail, it must be noted, are virtues anyhow, superiorities that count in peaceful as well as in military competition; but the strain on them, being infinitely intenser in the latter case, makes war infinitely more searching as a trial. No ordeal is comparable to its winnowings. Its dread hammer is the welder of men into cohesive states, and nowhere but in such states can human nature adequately develop its capacity. The only alternative is "degeneration."

Dr. Steinmetz is a conscientious thinker, and his book, short as it is, takes much into account. Its upshot can, it seems to me, be summed up in Simon Patten's word, that mankind was nursed in pain and fear, and that the transition to a "pleasure-economy" may be fatal to a being wielding no powers of defense against its disintegrative influences. If we speak of the *fear of emancipation from the fear-regime*, we put the whole situation into a single phrase; fear regarding ourselves now taking the place of the ancient fear of the enemy.

Turn the fear over as I will in my mind, it all seems to lead back to two unwillingnesses of the imagination, one aesthetic, and the other moral; unwillingness, first to envisage a future in which army-life, with its many elements of charm, shall be forever impossible, and in which the destinies of peoples shall nevermore be decided quickly, thrillingly, and tragically, by force, but only gradually and insipidly by "evolution"; and, secondly, unwillingness to see the supreme theatre of human strenuousness closed, and the splendid military aptitudes of men doomed to keep always in a state of latency and never show themselves in action. These insistent unwillingnesses, no less than other aesthetic and ethical insistencies, have, it seems to me, to be listened to and respected. One cannot meet them effectively by mere counter-insistency on war's expensiveness and horror. The horror makes the thrill; and when the question is of getting the extremest and supremest out of human nature, talk of expense sounds ignominious. The weakness of so much merely negative criticism is evident—pacifism makes no converts from the military party. The military party denies neither the bestiality nor

---

*Schiller, "History Is the Last Judgment" (ed.'s note).

the horror, nor the expense; it only says that these things tell but half the story. It only says that war is *worth* them; that, taking human nature as a whole, its wars are its best protection against its weaker and more cowardly self, and that mankind cannot *afford* to adopt a peace-economy.

Pacificists ought to enter more deeply into the aesthetical and ethical point of view of their opponents. Do that first in any controversy, says J. J. Chapman, *then move the point*, and your opponent will follow. So long as anti-militarists propose no substitute for war's disciplinary function, no *moral equivalent* of war, analogous, as one might say, to the mechanical equivalent of heat, so long they fail to realize the full inwardness of the situation. And as a rule they do fail. The duties, penalties, and sanctions pictured in the utopias they paint are all too weak and tame to touch the military-minded. Tolstoi's pacificism is the only exception to this rule, for it is profoundly pessimistic as regards all this world's values, and makes the fear of the Lord furnish the moral spur provided elsewhere by the fear of the enemy. But our socialistic peace-advocates all believe absolutely in this world's values; and instead of the fear of the Lord and the fear of the enemy, the only fear they reckon with is the fear of poverty if one be lazy. This weakness pervades all the socialistic literature with which I am acquainted. Even in Lowes Dickinson's exquisite dialogue,[1] high wages and short hours are the only forces invoked for overcoming man's distaste for repulsive kinds of labor. Meanwhile men at large still live as they always have lived, under a pain-and-fear economy— for those of us who live in an ease-economy are but an island in the stormy ocean—and the whole atmosphere of present-day utopian literature tastes mawkish and dishwatery to people who still keep a sense for life's more bitter flavors. It suggests, in truth, ubiquitous inferiority.

Inferiority is always with us, and merciless scorn of it is the keynote of the military temper. "Dogs, would you live forever?" shouted Frederick the Great. "Yes," say our utopians, "let us live forever, and raise our level gradually." The best thing about our "inferiors" to-day is that they are as tough as nails, and physically and morally almost as insensitive. Utopianism would see them soft and squeamish, while militarism would keep their callousness, but transfigure it into a meritorious characteristic, needed by "the service," and redeemed by that from the suspicion of inferiority. All the qualities of a man acquire dignity when he knows that the service of the collectivity that owns him needs them. If proud of the collectivity, his own pride rises in proportion. No collectivity is like

[1] "Justice and Liberty," New York, 1909.

an army for nourishing such pride; but it has to be confessed that the only sentiment which the image of pacific cosmopolitan industrialism is capable of arousing in countless worthy breasts is shame at the idea of belonging to *such* a collectivity. It is obvious that the United States of America as they exist to-day impress a mind like General Lea's as so much human blubber. Where is the sharpness and precipitousness, the contempt for life, whether one's own, or another's? Where is the savage "yes" and "no," the unconditional duty? Where is the conscription? Where is the blood-tax? Where is anything that one feels honored by belonging to?

Having said thus much in preparation, I will now confess my own utopia. I devoutly believe in the reign of peace and in the gradual advent of some sort of a socialistic equilibrium. The fatalistic view of the war-function is to me nonsense, for I know that war-making is due to definite motives and subject to prudential checks and reasonable criticisms, just like any other form of enterprise. And when whole nations are the armies, and the science of destruction vies in intellectual refinement with the sciences of production, I see that war becomes absurd and impossible from its own monstrosity. Extravagant ambitions will have to be replaced by reasonable claims, and nations must make common cause against them. I see no reason why all this should not apply to yellow as well as to white countries, and I look forward to a future when acts of war shall be formally outlawed as between civilized peoples.

All these beliefs of mine put me squarely into the anti-militarist party. But I do not believe that peace either ought to be or will be permanent on this globe, unless the states pacifically organized preserve some of the old elements of army-discipline. A permanently successful peace-economy cannot be a simple pleasure-economy. In the more or less socialistic future towards which mankind seems drifting we must still subject ourselves collectively to those severities which answer to our real position upon this only partly hospitable globe. We must make new energies and hardihoods continue the manliness to which the military mind so faithfully clings. Martial virtues must be the enduring cement; intrepidity, contempt of softness, surrender of private interest, obedience to command, must still remain the rock upon which states are built—unless, indeed, we wish for dangerous reactions against commonwealths fit only for contempt, and liable to invite attack whenever a center of crystallization for military-minded enterprise gets formed anywhere in their neighborhood.

The war-party is assuredly right in affirming and reaffirming that the martial virtues, although originally gained by the race through war, are absolute and permanent human goods. Patriotic pride and ambition in their military form are, after all, only specifications of a more general competitive passion. They are its first form, but that is no reason for supposing them to be its last form. Men now are proud of belonging to a conquering nation, and without a murmur they lay down their persons and their wealth, if by so doing they may fend off subjection. But who can be sure that *other aspects of one's country* may not, with time and education and suggestion enough, come to be regarded with similarly effective feelings of pride and shame? Why should men not some day feel that it is worth a blood-tax to belong to a collectivity superior in *any* ideal respect? Why should they not blush with indignant shame if the community that owns them is vile in any way whatsoever? Individuals, daily more numerous, now feel this civic passion. It is only a question of blowing on the spark till the whole population gets incandescent, and on the ruins of the old morals of military honor, a stable system of morals of civic honor builds itself up. What the whole community comes to believe in grasps the individual as in a vise. The war-function has grasped us so far; but constructive interests may some day seem no less imperative, and impose on the individual a hardly lighter burden.

Let me illustrate my idea more concretely. There is nothing to make one indignant in the mere fact that life is hard, that men should toil and suffer pain. The planetary conditions once for all are such, and we can stand it. But that so many men, by mere accidents of birth and opportunity, should have a life of *nothing else* but toil and pain and hardness and inferiority imposed upon them, should have *no* vacation, while others natively no more deserving never get any taste of this campaigning life at all,—*this* is capable of arousing indignation in reflective minds. It may end by seeming shameful to all of us that some of us have nothing but campaigning, and others nothing but unmanly ease. If now—and this is my idea—there were, instead of military conscription a conscription of the whole youthful population to form for a certain number of years a part of the army enlisted against *Nature*, the injustice would tend to be evened out, and numerous other goods to the commonwealth would follow. The military ideals of hardihood and discipline would be wrought into the growing fiber of the people; no one would remain blind as the luxurious classes now are blind, to man's relations to the globe he lives on, and to the permanently sour and hard foundations of his higher life. To coal and iron mines, to freight trains, to fishing fleets in December, to dishwashing, clothes-washing, and window-washing, to road-building and tunnel-making, to foundries and stoke-holes, and to the frames of skyscrapers, would our gilded youths be drafted off, according to their choice, to get the childishness knocked out of them, and to come back into society with healthier sympathies and soberer ideas. They would have paid their blood-tax, done their own part in the immemorial human warfare against nature; they would tread the earth more proudly, the women would value them more highly, they would be better fathers and teachers of the following generation.

Such a conscription, with the state of public opinion that would have required it, and the many moral fruits it would bear, would preserve in the midst of a pacific civilization the manly virtues which the military party is so afraid of seeing disappear in peace. We should get toughness without callousness, authority with as little criminal cruelty as possible, and painful work done cheerily because the duty is temporary, and threatens not, as now, to degrade the whole remainder of one's life. I spoke of the "moral equivalent" of war. So far, war has been the only force that can discipline a whole community, and until an equivalent discipline is organized, I believe that war must have its way. But I have no serious doubt that the ordinary prides and shames of social man, once developed to a certain intensity, are capable of organizing such a moral equivalent as I have sketched, or some other just as effective for preserving manliness of type. It is but a question of time, of skilful propagandism, and of opinion-making men seizing historic opportunities.

The martial type of character can be bred without war. Strenuous honor and disinterestedness abound elsewhere. Priests and medical men are in a fashion educated to it, and we should all feel some degree of it imperative if we were conscious of our work as an obligatory service to the state. We should be *owned*, as soldiers are by the army, and our pride would rise accordingly. We could be poor, then, without humiliation, as army officers now are. The only thing needed henceforward is to inflame the civic temper as past history has inflamed the military temper. H. G. Wells, as usual, sees the center of the situation. "In many ways," he says,

Military organization is the most peaceful of activities. When the contemporary man steps from the street, of clamorous insincere advertisement, push, adulteration, underselling and intermittent employment into the barrack-yard, he steps on to a higher social plane, into an atmosphere of service and cooperation and of infinitely more honorable emulations. Here at least men are not flung out of employment to degenerate because there is no immediate work for them to do. They are fed and drilled and trained for better services. Here at least a man is supposed to win promotion by self-forgetfulness and not by self-seeking. And beside the feeble and irregular endowment of research by commercialism, its little short-sighted snatches at profit by innovation and scientific economy, see how remarkable is the steady and rapid development of method and appliances in naval and military affairs! Nothing is more striking than to compare the progress of civil conveniences which has been left almost entirely to the trader, to the progress in military apparatus during the last few decades. The house-appliances of to-day, for example, are little better than they were fifty years ago. A house of to-day is still almost as ill-ventilated, badly heated by wasteful fires, clumsily arranged and furnished as the house of 1858. Houses a couple of hundred years old are still satisfactory places of residence, so little have our standards risen. But the rifle or battleship of fifty years ago was beyond all comparison inferior to those we possess; in power, in speed, in convenience alike. No one has a use now for such superannuated things. [2]

Wells adds [3] that he thinks that the conceptions of order and discipline, the tradition of service and devotion, of physical fitness, unstinted exertion, and universal responsibility, which universal military duty is now teaching European nations, will remain a permanent acquisition, when the last ammunition has been used in the fireworks that celebrate the final peace. I believe as he does. It would be simply preposterous if the only force that could work ideals of honor and standards of efficiency into English or American natures should be the fear of being killed by the Germans or the Japanese. Great indeed is Fear; but it is not, as our military enthusiasts believe and try to make us believe, the only stimulus known for awakening the higher ranges of men's spiritual energy. The amount of alteration in public opinion which my utopia postulates is vastly less than the difference between the mentality of those black warriors who pursued Stanley's party on the Congo with their cannibal war-cry of "Meat! Meat!" and that of the "general-staff" of any civilized nation. History has seen the latter interval bridged over: the former one can be bridged over much more easily.

[2]"First and Last Things," 1908, p. 215.
[3]*Ibid.*, p. 226.

John C. Ford, S.J.

The Morality of
Obliteration Bombing

The Moral Problem Raised by Obliteration Bombing

I do not intend to discuss here the question: Can any modern war be morally justified? The overwhelming majority of Catholic theologians would answer, I am sure, that there can be a justifiable modern war. And the practically unanimous voice of American Catholicism, including that of the hierarchy, assures us that we are fighting a just war at present. I accept that position. Our question deals rather with the morality of a given means made use of in the prosecution of a war which itself is justified.

However, it cannot be denied that this question leads us close to the more general one as to the possibility of a just modern war; for obliteration bombing includes the bombing of civilians, and is a practice which can be called typical of "total" war. If it is a necessary part of total war, and if all modern war must be total, then a condemnation of obliteration bombing would logically lead to a condemnation of all modern war. With Father Ulpian Lopez, of the Gregorian University, I do not intend to go that far. I believe that it is possible for modern war to be waged within the limits set by the laws of morality, and that the resort to obliteration bombing is not an essential part of it, even when war is waged against an enemy who has no scruples in the matter. But I call attention to the close connection between the two questions to show that I am not unaware of the implications. If anyone were to declare that modern war is necessarily total, and necessarily involves direct attack on the life of innocent civilians, and, therefore, that obliteration bombing is justified, my reply would be: So much the worse for modern war. If it necessarily includes such means, it is necessarily immoral itself.

Father Ford is professor emeritus of moral theology at Weston College in Weston, Massachusetts. Before retirement he was on the faculty of Catholic University. He has written widely in the field of moral theology. His most significant publication is the two volume work *Contemporary Moral Theology,* written in collaboration with Gerald Kelley (Vol. One, 1958; Vol. Two, 1963).

His article "The Morality of Obliteration Bombing" appeared in *Theological Studies,* Vol. 5 (1944), pp. 261-309. The portions included here are from pp. 267-271, 280-305, and are reprinted with the permission of the author and Theological Studies, Inc. The footnotes have been renumbered and in a few cases abridged.

The morality of obliteration bombing can be looked at from the point of view of the bombardier who asks in confession whether he may execute the orders of his military leaders, or it may be looked at from the viewpoint of the leaders who are responsible for the adoption of obliteration bombing as a recognized instrument of the general strategy of war. The present paper takes the latter viewpoint. It is not aimed at settling difficulties of the individual soldier's conscience.

Of course, there is an unavoidable logical connection between the morality of the whole plan and the morality of the act of the bombardier who executes the plan. If the plan is immoral, the execution of it is immoral. And nobody is allowed to execute orders to do something intrinsically wrong on the plea that he did it under orders. But when the priest in the confessional is presented with a comparatively new problem like this one—a problem which may involve tremendous upheavals in the consciences of many individuals, and on which ecclesiastical authorities have not laid down definite norms—he will necessarily hesitate before refusing absolution. When he has, besides, a well-established rule based on the presumption which favors civil authorities, and which in ordinary cases justifies subordinates in carrying out orders, his hesitation will increase. I believe that as far as confessional practice is concerned, the rule I suggested in 1941 (before we entered the war) is a safe one: "The application of our moral principles to modern war leaves so much to be desired that we are not in a position to impose obligations on the conscience of the individual, whether he be a soldier with a bayonet, or a conscientious objector, *except in the cases where violation of natural law is clear.*"[1] A clear violation of natural law can be known to the ordinary individual soldier in a case of this kind through the definite pronouncement of the Church, or of the hierarchy, or even through a consensus of moral theologians over a period of time. On the question of obliteration bombing we have no such norms. The present article obviously does not supply the need. Hence, I believe the confessor is justified in absolving the bombardier who feels forced to carry out orders to take part in obliteration bombing, unless the penitent himself is convinced (as I am) of the immorality of the practice.

The present paper attempts to deal with the problem on a larger scale. The Popes have condemned as immoral some of the procedures of modern war, but they have abstained, as far as I know, from using terms which would put a clear, direct burden on the conscience of the individual subordinate in a new matter like the present one. Later on I shall attempt to show that obliteration

1"Current Moral Theology," *Theological Studies,* II (Dec. 1941), p. 556.

bombing must be one of the procedures which Pius XII has condemned as immoral. But my viewpoint at present is that of one trying to solve the general moral problem, not of teaching confessors at what point they must draw the line and refuse absolution. Incidentally, I do not believe a discussion of probabilism, or of what is probably allowable in this matter of bombing, would be fruitful, once one takes the larger point of view. Probabilism is the necessary resort of those who cannot find the truth with certainty, and yet must act. In confessional practice one must rely on it in some form or other. But to approach a major moral question probabilistically would be to confess at the start that the truth is unattainable. Such a state of mind would not be likely to contribute to the science of morality. My object is to make the small beginning of such a contribution.

The principal moral problem raised by obliteration bombing, then, is that of the rights of non-combatants to their lives in war time. Rights are protected by laws. The laws in question are the international law, the law of humanity, and the natural law. These distinct names are heard continually, especially in the documents of the present Pope.[2] But they do not always stand for distinct things. Sometimes international law coincides with and reinforces natural law, or the laws of humanity. And so of the others. The ideas often overlap. But, insofar as they are distinct from one another, that distinction may be briefly indicated and illustrated as follows.

The rights which are protected by mere international law, are derived from positive compacts or treaties between governments, binding in justice, but ceasing to bind when the other party to the contract has ceased to observe it. For instance, certain laws that deal in detail with the treatment to be accorded prisoners are in this category. (I do not mean to imply that a single breach of an international engagement, or of a part of one, by one of the governments immediately releases the other government from all its contractual obligations to the first.)

The laws of humanity are rather vague norms based on more or less universal feelings of what decency, or fair play, or an educated human sympathy demand, but not based on compacts, and not clearly—as to particulars at any rate—contained within the dictates of the natural law. And sometimes the laws of humanity mean the laws of Christian charity, made known to us through the Christian revelation and exemplified in the life of Jesus Christ. For instance, the use of poison gas, or the spreading of disease germs among enemy combatants, if not forbidden already by international law, would be forbidden at least by the laws of humanity. It is not so

---

[2]Cf. *Principles for Peace* (Washington: N.C.W.C., 1943), passim.

clear, though, that such methods of putting the enemy soldiers out of the fight would be against the natural law.

I say that this is an example of what is meant by the law of humanity, insofar as this law is distinct from natural or international law. Actually, when the laws of humanity are mentioned, some precept of natural law is often involved. And it has been the task of international law, too, under the nourishing influence of the Christian religion, to protect the natural rights of combatants and non-combatants alike. International agreements have led to a clarification of natural precepts, and made certain what the laws of humanity would leave uncertain, and made definite and particular what the law of nature contained only in a general way. The widespread abandonment of international law which characterizes the conduct of total war, the retrogression towards barbarism in every direction, is one of the most frightening developments in modern times. It is a disease that can destroy civilization.[3]

The present paper, though not excluding considerations based on international law and the law of humanity, will deal principally with the natural-law rights of non-combatants.[4] And our chief concern will be the right of the non-combatant to life and limb. His right not to have his property taken or destroyed (or his family torn asunder) is also pertinent, but will be mentioned only incidentally. Hence, we can put the moral problem raised by obliteration bombing in the form of the following questions, which the rest of the paper will try to answer:

1.   Do the majority of civilians in a modern nation at war enjoy a natural-law right of immunity from violent repression?

2.   Does obliteration bombing necessarily involve a violation of the rights of innocent civilians? . . .

[3]On this point Guido Gonella writes eloquently in *A World to Reconstruct* (Milwaukee: Bruce, 1944), Chap. XII.

[4]Discussion of the morality of obliteration bombing became widespread in this country with the publication of Vera Brittain's "Massacre by Bombing" in *Fellowship*, X (March 1944), p. 50. The article consisted of extracts from a book which appeared in England under the title *Seed of Chaos*. A similar but much briefer article by R. Alfred Hassler, "Slaughter of the Innocent," had appeared in *Fellowship*, February 1944. The reception accorded Vera Brittain's sober recital of facts and moral arguments is described by James M. Gillis in "Editorial Comment," *Catholic World*, CLIX (May 1944), p. 97, who believes that obliteration, on Catholic principles, is clearly immoral. But both the facts and the moral *status quaestionis* of Miss Brittain's article were almost universally ignored or misrepresented by the press. There was an almost complete evasion of the moral issues involved. Even the President's reply, made through Mr. Early, is well characterized by the author herself as "irrelevant, unjustified, and destructive of the very ideals with which the American people went to war" ("Not Made in Germany," *Fellowship*, X, June 1944, p. 106).

The Contemporary Question of Fact

... It is obvious ... that the conditions of modern war are changed, and the change makes it very difficult and sometimes impossible to draw accurately the line which separates combatants from innocent non-combatants according to natural law. Soldiers under arms are obviously combatants. It is not so clear what is to be said of civilian munitions workers, the members of various organized labor battalions not under arms, and so of others. Of these doubtful classes I do not intend to speak. In the end, only new international agreements will effectively and precisely protect the rights of these groups.

But it is not necessary to draw an accurate line in order to solve the problem of obliteration bombing. It is enough to show that there are large numbers of people even in the conditions of modern warfare who are clearly to be classed as innocent non-combatants, and then that, wherever the line is drawn, obliteration bombing goes beyond it and violates the rights of these people. It seems to me that an unnecessary attitude of defeat is betrayed by writers like Dr. McReavy, who seem to think that, because we do not know exactly where to draw the line, therefore we have to act as if there were no line at all between innocence and guilt (and hence find some other ground for protecting civilians from savagery). I think it is a fairly common fallacy in legal and moral argumentation to conclude that all is lost because there is a field of uncertainty to which our carefully formulated moral principles cannot be applied with precision.[5] It seems to me, furthermore, that this mentality is encouraged if one is taking the view of a confessor who thinks in terms of absolution for the individual penitent, and who naturally does not want to deny it unless he is certain that he has to. Finally, in this present matter, I think this defeatist mentality is encouraged in moralists who, as it were, have been put on the defensive by public, "patriotic," and official opinion, and overwhelmed with talk of the radically changed conditions of modern war—as if everything were now changed, and all or almost all civilians now played a direct part in the war, and as if in the past, when the classical formulas were put together, the civilians who were declared untouchable in those formulas had little or nothing to do with the war effort of their countries. Is it not evident that the most radical and significant change of all in modern warfare is not the increased co-operation of

---

[5]We do not talk this way in the matter of the absolutely grave sum, even though it is impossible to draw the line with precision. Even in philosophy, when determining what is a miracle, we admit we do not know how far nature can go, but we are sure of some things that are beyond her powers.

civilians behind the lines with the armed forces, but the enormously increased power of the armed forces to reach behind the lines and attack civilians indiscriminately, whether they are thus co-operating or not?

And so the question arises, who has the burden of proof—the civilian behind the lines, who clings to his traditional immunity, or the military leader with new and highly destructive weapons in his hands, who claims that he can attack civilians because modern industrial and economic conditions have changed the nature of war radically and made them all aggressors. Do we start with the supposition that the whole population of the enemy is presumably guilty, and that anyone who wants to exempt a group from that condemnation is called upon to prove the innocence of the group? Or do we start with the view that only armed soldiers are guilty combatants, and anyone who wants to increase the number of the guilty, and make unarmed civilians legitimate objects of violent repression, has the duty of proving his position? Is it not reasonable to put the burden of proof on those who are innovators? Do we not start from here: "Thou shalt not kill"? Seeing that the wartime rights of civilians to life and property are declared by centuries of tradition to be sacrosanct, what do we presume: a man's right to his life, even in war time, or my right to kill him? his right to his property, or my right to destroy it? Not merely the conscience of humanity, not merely international law, but the teaching of Catholic theologians for centuries, the voice of the Church speaking through her Councils and through her hierarchy and through the Supreme Pontiff down to the present day, uniformly insist on the innocence and consequent immunity of civil populations. It is obviously the burden of those who think that distinction invalid (or, what comes to the same thing, completely impractical) to prove their contention. I can understand how a confessor, with thoughts of probabilism running through his head, would feel that when he refuses absolution he has the burden of showing he has a right to refuse it. But I cannot understand a moralist taking that point of view with regard to the rights of civilians. He has not the burden of proving these rights. On the contrary, those who want to increase the number of combatants, and include large numbers, even the "vast majority," of the civilian population amongst the guilty, must justify themselves.

The principal justifications I have seen are worthless. They say: the enemy did it first; or, military necessity demands it; or, it is justified by way of reprisal; or, the present situation is desperately abnormal (as if there were ever a war which was not); or, nowadays the whole nation takes part in the aggression, whereas formerly it was only army against army. As to this last point, it is true that the number of civilians who contribute immediately to the armed prosecution of the war has increased in modern times, but to say that all or nearly all do so is a grave distortion of the facts, as we shall see. And to imply that in the past the general civilian population co-operated not at all or only negligibly is equally far from the facts. Armies in the past had to be supplied with food, clothing, guns, and ammunition, and it was the civilian population who supplied them. The Church and the theologians in declaring civilians innocent realized very well that even in former times civilian sympathies, their moral support, and their actual physical aid went to further the cause of their country.

Perhaps the governments would like to enlist the active and immediate participation of all civilians in the war itself; but even this is doubtful. And the fact is that they do not succeed in doing so, and from the very nature of the case cannot. Even in a modern war there remains necessarily a vast field of civilian work and activity which is remote from the armed prosecution of the war.

Let us see for a moment what the abandonment of the distinction between combatants and non-combatants would mean in practice; or what it would mean to say that hardly any civilians are innocent in a modern war, because all are co-operating in the aggression. It would mean, for instance, that all the persons listed below are guilty, and deserve death, or at least are fit objects of violent repression. I should not inflict this long list on my readers (though I really believe one can profit by its careful perusal), unless I were convinced that some have been misled by the propaganda of total-war-mongers, or have taken uncritically at their face value statements about "a nation in arms," or "all co-operate in the aggression," or "the enemy has mobilized the whole population," or "nobody is innocent except the infant." Read the list. If you can believe that these classes of persons deserve to be described as combatants, or deserve to be treated as legitimate objects of violent repression, then I shall not argue further. If, when their governments declare war, these persons are so guilty that they deserve death, or almost any violence to person and property short of death, then let us forget the law of Christian charity, the natural law, and go back to barbarism, admitting that total war has won out and we must submit to it. The list:

Farmers, fishermen, foresters, lumberjacks, dressmakers, milliners, bakers, printers, textile workers, millers, painters, paper hangers, piano tuners, plasterers, shoemakers, cobblers, tailors, upholsterers, furniture makers, cigar and cigarette makers, glove makers, hat makers, suit makers, food processors, dairymen, fish canners, fruit and vegetable canners, slaughterers and packers, sugar refiners, liquor and beverage workers, teamsters, garage help, telephone girls, advertising men, bankers, brokers, clerks in stores, commercial travelers, decorators, window dressers, deliverymen, inspectors, insurance agents, retail dealers, salesmen and saleswomen in all trades, undertakers, wholesale dealers, meatcutters, butchers, actors, architects, sculptors, artists, authors, editors, reporters, priests, laybrothers, nuns, seminarians, professors, school teachers, dentists, lawyers, judges, musicians, photographers, physicians, surgeons, trained nurses, librarians, social and welfare workers, Red Cross workers, religious workers, theatre owners, technicians, laboratory assistants, barbers, bootblacks, charwomen, cleaners and dyers, hotelmen, elevator tenders, housekeepers, janitors, sextons, domestic servants, cooks, maids, nurses, handymen, laundry operatives, porters, victuallers, bookkeepers, accountants, statisticians, cashiers, stenographers, secretaries, typists, all office help, mothers of families, patients in hospitals, prison inmates, prison guards, institutional inmates, old men and women, all children with the use of reason, i.e., from seven years up. (After all, these latter buy war stamps, write letters of encouragement to their brothers in the service, and even carry the dinner pail to the father who works in the aircraft factory. They all co-operate in some degree in the aggression.)[6]

Do these persons, whom I consider to be, almost without exception, *certainly innocent non-combatants according to natural law*, constitute a large proportion of the general civilian population? Here again, though it is impossible to give accurate figures for the proportion, it can be maintained with complete certitude that they constitute the vast majority of the entire civil population even in war time. In an industrial country like the United States they represent at least three-quarters of the total civil population, and probably much more. In other countries the proportion would vary according to the degree of industrialization and militarization, but I am convinced that even in the most totally war-minded country in the world the certainly innocent civilians far outnumber those whose status could be considered doubtful.

This estimate of three-quarters can be arrived at in various ways. For instance, the total estimated population of continental United States in 1944 could be placed roughly at 135 millions. An estimate of the armed forces is 11 millions. This leaves a civilian population of 124 millions. (The government census estimated the civilian

[6]Note also that the civilian populations of neutral countries are also aggressors on this theory—for they supply food and raw materials to the enemy—and so on *ad infinitum*. Another point to be remembered is that when strategic air blows are struck at the very beginning of a war, the populations that feel their heavy weight have not had time to become guilty aggressors.

population as of March 1, 1943, at more than 128 millions.) Of these 124 millions, it would be a very generous estimate that would place the number of those engaged in war work and essential work (manufactures immediately connected with the violent prosecution of the war, mining, transportation, communications, and even public offices close to the war) at 31 millions of people, that is, one-quarter of the whole civilian population.

I call this a generous estimate for the following reasons. In 1930, when our total population (continental United States) was about 123 millions, the census showed about 49 million persons over 10 years of age gainfully employed. Of these only about 15 millions at the most could be considered as working in industries, manufacturing, and other occupations, which in case of war would become connected closely with the prosecution of the war. It might be argued that at the present time these occupations have more than doubled their numbers, but this would be to forget that the general population has also increased 12 millions meanwhile, and that furthermore a very large number of the 11 million service men have been recruited from these same manufacturing and war industries.

Another approach is to take the total population in 1945, roughly estimated at 136 millions, and subtract from it, first, an estimated army and navy of 12 millions. Of the 124 million civilians left, 68 millions are women, 16 millions are male children under 14 years of age, and more than four and one-half millions are men over 65 years of age. Thus the civilian population of 124 millions contains 88 millions of women, children, and old men. Of course, some (a few millions perhaps?) of these women make munitions and do other war work, as do also some of the old men. They also take part in transportation and communications and other "essential" work. But many more millions of men are not in war work. And making all due allowance, it still seems to be a very safe estimate that at least three-quarters of the civilian population are in no sense giving such immediate co-operation to the armed prosecution of the war that they can be considered combatants, or guilty of aggression, or deserving of violent repression. Further statistics with regard to industrial cities, which will be given later, will confirm this general estimate.

The conclusion of this section of our paper is an answer to the question: Do the majority of civilians in a modern nation at war enjoy a natural-law right of immunity from violent repression? The answer is an emphatic affirmative. The great majority, at least three-quarters in a country like the United States, have such a right.

Now let us proceed to consider whether obliteration bombing, as carefully defined above, violates the rights of innocent non-combatants.

I have defined obliteration bombing as follows: *It is the strategic bombing, by means of incendiaries and explosives, of industrial centers of population, in which the target to be wiped out is not a definite factory, bridge, or similar object, but a large section of a whole city, comprising one-third to two-thirds of its whole built-up area, and including by design the residential districts of workingmen and their families.* It is perfectly obvious that such bombing necessarily includes an attack on the lives, health, and property of many innocent civilians. Above I estimated that at the very least three-quarters of the civilian population in a country like the United States must be classed as certainly innocent civilians, and immune from attack. That estimate applied to the general population and was an extremely modest one. But even in industrial cities in war time there is a very large proportion of the civil population which it would be certainly immoral to attack—most women, almost all children under 14 years, almost all men over seventy, and a very large number of men who are engaged neither in war manufactures, transport, communications, nor in other doubtful categories. At least two-thirds and probably more are certainly to be classed among the innocent—an estimate based on figures supplied by statisticians of the War Manpower Commission.

For instance, in July, 1944, the Boston Labor Market Area had a total population of about 1,800,000. Of these, the War Manpower Commission estimates that only about 800,000 are gainfully employed, i.e., much less than fifty per cent. Now I feel sure that very few people who are not gainfully employed at all can be classed as proximate co-operators in the armed prosecution of the war. And of those who are employed, a very large number are only remotely connected with the war effort. A statistician connected with the Commission estimates that out of the 800,000 we should consider only about 300,000 as essential war workers. The other 500,000 have been called "less essential" because their connection with the war is more remote. Even the classification "essential" would probably include many persons, such as textile workers making Army cloth and uniforms, etc., who are far from being engaged in violent warlike action.[7]

---

[7]The above estimate does not take into account Army and Navy personnel within the area. Statistics on that point are naturally unavailable, but we should remember that only about 8% of the total U.S. population is in uniform, and that the above area has no large troop concentrations included in the rough estimate of its total population.

Making due allowance for government officials, semi-military personnel, such as air-raid wardens, WAVES, WACS, etc., it is very conservative to say that at least two-thirds of the total population of the Boston area is so remotely connected with the violent prosecution of the war that no stretching of terms or principles could make them legitimate objects of violent repression.

If Boston were subject to obliteration attack, not all the area would become a target. But the principal, more densely populated parts of it would, e.g., North End, South End, West End, East Boston, South Boston, Dorchester, Charlestown, Everett, Chelsea, Brighton, parts of Brookline, Cambridge, Hingham, Quincy, etc. Perhaps the number of munitions workers and "warlike" workers in these districts forms a higher percentage. It is impossible to find out. (Nor would the Germans bother to find out if they could take up obliteration bombing against us, as we have against them.) In any event, to say that two-thirds of the civil population liable to this kind of bombing is innocent is to make a conservative estimate.

In the Worcester Labor Market Area the total population in 1940 was about 260,000. This had increased, I believe, by 1943; but let us imagine it was about the same (since this works against us). The total of employed persons in the area in September, 1943, after we had been at war almost two years, was about 91,000. This means that far less than half of this highly industrial area was gainfully employed. Even in the city of Worcester itself, in 1943, the War Production Board estimated that only seventy-five per cent of the manufacturing employees were in war manufacturing.[8] I would estimate, on the basis of figures supplied by government statisticians, that of the total employed in the area (91,000), at least 30,000 to 35,000 could be classed as certainly not connected proximately with the violent prosecution of the war. This means—again making all due allowance for service men, government officials, transport, communications and utilities workers—that at the very least two-thirds of the civil population must be classed as certainly innocent according to theological standards.[9]

---

[8]*An Analysis of Post War Economic Conditions in Worcester* (Worcester: Worcester Chamber of Commerce, 1943), p. 5. On p. 15, the estimate is made that, in 1939, 7.8% of the whole U.S. population was engaged in manufacturing, while 13.7% of the Worcester area population was thus engaged.

[9]This estimate is for the *certainly* innocent. It must not be forgotten that many of the others are probably innocent according to natural law, or at least probably immune from attack because of international agreements still in effect. Since I have promised not to discuss probabilism in this connection, I merely ask: Have these groups a *certain* right to be deprived of life, family, and property until their combatant or guilty status is proved with certainty?

And lest anyone be surprised at this result, we should always remember that fifty per cent of the population throughout the United States is female, and about fifteen per cent are male children and old men. Facts and common sense tell us to guard carefully against the total-war fallacy that the whole nation is arrayed in arms against the whole enemy nation.

These figures are for typical centers of industry in the United States. What the figures would be in Germany no one can tell. But even in Germany in 1939 only about one-half of the total population was listed by the census as gainfully employed. And of these almost one-half were engaged in agriculture, trade, and domestic service. Allowing for higher percentages in the industrial centers (comparable to Boston and Worcester), now that the war has been going on five years, we are still safe in estimating that the majority of the inhabitants even in the centers of war production marked for devastation and obliteration are innocent civilians.[10]

The principle of the double effect   And so the immorality of obliteration bombing, its violation of the rights of these innocent civilians to life, bodily integrity, and property would be crystal clear, and would not be subject to dispute, at least amongst Catholics, were it not for the appeal to the principle of the double effect. This principle can be worded as follows: The foreseen evil effect of a man's action is not morally imputable to him, provided that (1) the action in itself is directed immediately to some other result, (2) the evil effect is not willed either in itself or as a means to the other result, (3) the permitting of the evil effect is justified by reasons of proportionate weight.

Applying the principle to obliteration bombing, it would be argued: The bombing has a good effect, the destruction of war industries, communications, and military installations, leading to the defeat of the enemy; it also has an evil effect, the injury and death of innocent civilians (and the destruction of their property). The damage to civilian life (and property) is not intentional; it is not a means to the production of the good effect, but is merely its

---

[10]I have seen the statement made that 10% of the population of the Ruhr is engaged at least part time in air defense work. This would include, I suppose, both the military personnel and the civilian passive defense services. Spaight, *Bombing Vindicated*, p. 115, says: "All the civilians enrolled in the service of passive defense—the fire fighters, the fire-watchers, the rescue parties, the demolition squads—cannot be classed otherwise than as warriors," and hence are liable to direct lethal attack. The logic of total war is inexorable. I can set fire to your house. When your wife tries to put the fire out, she becomes a "warrior" and I can kill her. Spaight claims immunity for civilians who are not engaged in definitely warlike activities (p. 112), but in practice he extends warlike activity to include fire-watching and rescuing of the wounded.

incidental accompaniment. Furthermore, the slaughter, maiming, and destruction can be permitted because there are sufficiently weighty excusing causes, such as shortening the war, military necessity, saving our own soldiers' lives, etc. This viewpoint, therefore, would find a simple solution to the moral problem merely by advising the air strategist to let go his bombs, but withhold his intention. In what follows I shall attempt to show that this is an unwarranted application of the principle of the double effect.

The principle of the double effect, though basic in scientific Catholic morality, is not, however, a mathematical formula, nor an analytical principle. It is a practical formula which synthesizes an immense amount of moral experience, and serves as an efficient guide in countless perplexing cases. But just because it is called into play to solve the more difficult cases, it is liable to sophistical abuse. Some applications of it can only be called casuistical in the bad sense of that word.[11] It is a truism among moralists that, though the principle is clear in itself, its application requires "sound moral judgment." It seems to me that the following are the points which require a moral, rather than a mathematical or merely verbal, interpretation of the principle, when it is applied in practice.

First, when is it possible, psychologically and honestly, for one to avoid the direct willing of an evil effect immediately consequent upon one's action; or to put it another way, when can an action, estimated morally, be considered really twofold in its immediate efficiency? Secondly, when is the evil effect to be considered only incidental to the main result, and not a means made use of implicitly or explicitly to produce it? To arrive at a sound moral estimate in these matters, it is often helpful to consider the physical proximity of the good and evil effects, or the inevitable and immediate character of the evil effect in the physical order, to consider its extent or size by comparison with the good effect immediately produced, and to consider especially whether the evil effect *de facto* contributes to the ultimate good desired, even if not explicitly willed as a means. And, of course, a careful estimate must be made of the proportionate excusing cause, in the light of all the circumstances that have a bearing on the case. Perhaps this is only saying that without common sense the principle of the double effect may lead

---

[11]Even St. Thomas has been accused repeatedly of defending the subtle proposition: When you kill an unjust aggressor you merely permit his death while intending to save your own life. Vicente Alonso, *El principio del doble efecto en los commentadores de Santo Tomas* (Rome: Gregorian University Dissertation, 1937), has shown that in II-II, q. 64, a. 7, St. Thomas merely held that the killing of an unjust aggressor must be willed only as a means, not as an end in itself. St. Thomas did not know the principle of the double effect as we formulate it.

to casuistical conclusions; but I believe I am saying more than that. I am pointing out that the principle is not an ultimate guide in difficult cases, because it is only a practical formula and has to be applied by a hand well practiced in moral principles and moral solutions.

The question of intention   As to obliteration bombing, then, is it possible to employ this procedure without directly intending the damage to innocent civilians and their property? Obviously, the destruction of property is directly intended. The leaders acknowledge it as an objective. And on this score alone one could argue with reason against the morality of the practice. But since the property of civilians is not so absolutely immune as their persons and lives from direct attack in war time, I prefer to deal mainly with the latter.

Looking at obliteration bombing as it actually takes place, can we say that the maiming and death of hundreds of thousands of innocent persons, which are its immediate result, are not directly intended, but merely permitted? Is it possible psychologically and honestly for the leaders who have developed and ordered the employment of this strategy to say they do not intend any harm to innocent civilians? To many, I am sure, the distinction between the material fabric of a city, especially the densely populated residential areas, and the hundreds of thousands of human inhabitants of such areas, will seem very unreal and casuistical.[12] They will consider it merely playing with words to say that in dropping a bomb on a man's house, knowing he is there with his family, the intent is merely to destroy the house and interfere with enemy production (through absenteeism), while permitting the injury and death of the family.

Dr. John K. Ryan of Catholic University wrote on this point as follows (after the present war started, but before we entered it):

The actual physical situation in great modern cities is not such that they can be subjected to attack on the principle that only industrial, military, administrative and traffic centers are being attacked directly, while the damage done to

---

[12]"When the Germans launched their blitz on the English cities in 1940 there was a widespread and intense moral indignation at the volume of wholly indiscriminate slaughter and ruin which was only remotely and casuistically to be associated with attacks on ports or factories," says an editorial in *The London Tablet*, CLXXXIII (May 20, 1944), p. 243. The editorial goes on to say that conditions made it necessary for the British in their bombing to "widen the definition of the target to cover industrial areas and the dwellings of those who worked in the factories." The *Tablet* does not approve this, neither does it condemn it. I consider such "widening the definition of the target" to be a casuistical device.

noncombatants is only incidental and not an object of direct volition. Modern cities are not as compact and fortresslike as were those of the past. Their residential sections are so extensive, so clearly defined, and so discernible, that it is for the most part idle to attempt to apply the principle of indirection to attacks on these districts. Thus to rain explosives and incendiary bombs upon the vast residential tracts of say, Chicago, or Brooklyn, the Bronx, and the suburbs of New York City, on the score that this is only incidental to attack on munition plants and administrative headquarters in other parts of the city, cannot stand the slightest critical examination either moral or logic, as an instance of the principle of the double effect. In such an argument is contained the explicit distinction between groups and sections that may be made the object of direct attack and other groups and sections that are immune from such attack. But incendiary and explosive bombs would hardly respect this distinction, for they destroy with equal impartiality either group. When an entire city is destroyed by such means the military objectives are destroyed indirectly and incidentally as parts of a great civil center, rather than vice versa. It is a case of the good effect coming along with, or better, after and on account of the evil, instead of a case where the evil is incidental to the attainment of a good. . . . It is hardly correct to think and speak of the damage done to life and property in such situations as being 'incidental destruction.' Rather it is the realistic interpretation of this situation to hold that any good gained is incidental to the evil, and that the phrase 'wholesale destruction of property and civilian life' indicates the true relation between the good and evil effects involved. The evil effect is first, immediate and direct, while any military advantage comes through and after it in a secondary, derivative, and dependent way. As far as the principle of the double effect is concerned, an attack upon a large city with the weapons of modern warfare is the direct opposite of such an attack with the weapons of earlier days. . . . The general civil suffering from the immediate effects of total war cannot be justified on the score that it is indirect. Justification for the infliction of such suffering must be sought by other means, and it is doubtful if even war-time propaganda can present the new warfare as other than it is—a direct and intended offensive against the non-combatant population of the nations at war, especially as concentrated in large number in the great capital and industrial cities.[13]

[13]John K. Ryan, *Modern War and Basic Ethics,* pp. 105ff.

Obliteration bombing would come squarely under the condemnation of this argument.[14] It is enough to recall that in a single raid on Cologne (according to Mr. J. M. Spaight, one of the most enthusiastic and articulate defenders of the bombing), 5000 acres of the built-up part of the city were wiped out.[15] That means a territory eight miles square. And the American Army Air Forces' official story of the first year of bombing says of Hamburg: "Well over 2200 British and American aircraft dropped more than 7000 tons of high explosive and incendiaries on a city the size of Detroit. To quote an official report: 'There is nothing in the world to which this concentrated devastation of Hamburg can be compared, for an inferno of this scale in a town of this size has never been experienced, hardly even imagined, before.' "[16] The total weight of the bombs dropped on Hamburg in seven days equaled the tonnage dropped on London during the whole of the 1940-1941 blitz.[17] Mr. Spaight informs us: "What the effect was may be inferred from the ejaculations of one German radio commentator (Dr. Carl Hofman): 'Terror . . . terror . . . terror . . . pure, naked, bloody terror.' "[18]

More than nine square miles of Hamburg (77 per cent of its built-up area), including the largest workers' district in the city, were completely wiped out, according to British reports of the raids.[19] An RAF commentator said: "To all intents and purposes a city of 1,800,000 inhabitants lies in absolute ruins. . . . It is probably the most complete blotting-out of a city that ever happened."[20] This kind of thing is still going on. In July, 1944, General H. H. Arnold, commanding general of our Army Air Forces, announced that latest

---

[14]But I do not know Dr. Ryan's opinion on this present problem, which arose after he had written the above. To the casual, or even the careful reader of his book, it would appear that he did not believe in the possibility of a just modern war at all. But we know from his later repudiation of this thesis that it had never been his intention to defend it; cf. *Ecclesiastical Review*, CVIII (May 1943), p. 350.

[15] Spaight, *op. cit.*, p. 96.

[16]*Target: Germany*, p. 19.

[17]*Loc. cit.*

[18]Spaight, *op. cit.*, p. 89.

[19]Vera Brittain, "Massacre by Bombing," *Fellowship*, X (March 1944), p. 57.

[20]*Loc. cit.* Another RAF commentator said that "the greatest destruction from these raids has been to business and residential property, especially in the built-up area." Estimates of those killed varied from 65,000 to 200,000, but these figures have been questioned. Owing especially to phosphorus and incendiaries, Hamburg experts in charge of salvaging bodies believed that in the fire district only a very small percentage of the population, even those in shelters, escaped death

reports indicated that 40 to 50 per cent of the central portion of Berlin is "burned out. . . . Berlin is a ruined city." The bomber chief also stated that the Army Air Forces plan to continue their air offensive against Germany, "burning out" its industries and war centers.[21]

If these are the facts, what is to be said of the contention that the damage to civilian property and especially to civilian life is only incidental? Is it psychologically and honestly possible for the air strategist in circumstances like these to let go his bombs, and withhold his intention as far as the innocent are concerned? I have grave doubts of the possibility.

But there is another reason for excluding the possibility of such merely indirect intent. At the Casablanca conference, the combined chiefs of staff ordered a joint British-United States air offensive to accomplish "the progressive destruction and dislocation of the German military, industrial and economic system and *the under-mining of the morale of the German people* to the point where their capacity for armed resistance is fatally weakened."[22] *Target: Germany*, an official publication of the air forces, tells us that "the two bomber commands lost no time in setting about the job. To the RAF fell the task of destroying Germany's great cities, of silencing the iron heart-beat of the Ruhr, *of dispossessing the working population, of breaking the morale of the people*. The mission of VIII Bomber Command was the destruction of the key industries by which the German military machine was sustained."[23] This same authoritative publication (presented with a foreword by General Arnold himself) makes it clear that the terrorization of civilians is part of our bombing strategy. "Bombs behind the fighting fronts may rob armies of their vital supplies and make war so terrible that civilian populations will refuse to support the armed forces in the field. . . . *The physical attrition of warfare is no longer limited to the fighting forces.* Heretofore the home front has remained relatively secure; armies fought, civil populations worked and waited. This conflict's early air attacks were the first portents of a changing order." And after saying that we now follow the "bloody instructions" given us by the Nazis, and after describing the destruction of Hamburg and other industrial cities, this official account says: "Here, then, we have *terror and devastation* carried to the core of a warring nation."[24]

[21]*New York Times*, July 4, 1944.

[22]*Target: Germany*, p. 117 (italics added).

[23]*Loc. cit.*

[24]*Ibid.*, p. 19 (italics added). Charles J. V. Murphy denies the terror motive, saying that the real motive as to civilians is "to hound him with the multiplying incidents of catastrophe . . ." (*op. cit.*, p. 95).

Now I contend that it is impossible to make civilian terrorization, or the undermining of civilian morale, an object of bombing without having a direct intent to injure and kill civilians. The principal cause of civilian terror, the principal cause of the loss of morale, is the danger to life and limb which accompanies the raids. If one intends the end, terror, one cannot escape intending the principal means of obtaining that end, namely, the injury and death of civilians.

Both from the nature of the obliteration operation itself,[25] then, and from the professed objective of undermining morale, I conclude that it is impossible to adopt this strategy without having the direct intent of violating the rights of innocent civilians. This intent is, of course, gravely immoral.

On the question of direct intent it is well to remember, too, that it would be altogether naive to suppose that our military and political leaders were thinking in terms of a distinction between direct and indirect. Without impeaching their moral characters in the least, it is only common sense to recognize that their practical guiding norms in a matter of this kind are military necessity and political expediency. This is not to deny that they have consciences and follow them, but it is to doubt whether their consciences are sufficiently delicate to give them any trouble when this type of decision has to be made. When our forces bombed Rome, the officials took extreme care to hit only military objectives. And they took even greater care to broadcast the precautions they had taken, and to get statements from Catholic pilots defending the operation. Now if this solicitude has been due to a sincere regard for the morality of aiming at non-military targets, or for the necessity of avoiding direct intentional injury of the innocent, they would exercise the same care in every city they bombed, or at least in every comparable case. But I do not think it is cynical to believe that they were more interested in religious *feelings* and world reaction than they were in the morality of killing the innocent whether directly or indirectly, and of destroying non-military property. The present bombing of Germany confirms this view. From the moral point of view, the lives of the innocent inhabitants of Germany or any other

---

[25]Mr. Spaight's description of obliteration technique inadvertently confirms the view that a great deal more than the so-called target is really aimed at. Because precision work was not effective, "it was necessary to bring into use projectiles of such destructive capacity that when launched from great heights on the estimated target area they could be counted upon to wreck the target as well as (unfortunately) much else besides. The justification of the method must rest on military necessity." Actually this means that one aims at a whole area in order to get at a target. The destruction of the target is incidental to the destruction of the *estimated target area* (*Bombing Vindicated*, p. 98). On p. 97 he described the terrible "bomb-splash"; we do not know yet how devastating it is.

country are far more precious than the religious monuments of Rome, or the real estate of the Holy Father. But we hear nothing of a week's preliminary briefing to insure the safety of non-military targets in Berlin. We hear just the opposite. We hear the word obliterate.

Furthermore, we continually hear the argument: "They did it first," as a justification of our bombing of Germany. The argument is that since the Germans have attacked our innocent civilian populations on purpose, we can do the same thing to them.[26] Mr. Norman Cousins, editor of the *Saturday Review of Literature*, who has interested himself in the subject of obliteration bombing, apparently believes that any procedure whatever, no matter how brutal, is moral and legitimate for us to adopt once the enemy adopts it: "Once the enemy *starts* it [poison gas, and even, it seems, indiscriminate bacteriological warfare] it becomes no longer a moral but a military question, no longer a matter of argument but a matter of action."[27] Mr. Churchill's appeal to the popular revenge motive has been public.[28] At the present time there are numerous calls for revenge of the

---

[26]Mr. Spaight does not argue thus, however, in *Bombing Vindicated*. He claims that Germany never had a strategic bomber command and was seriously opposed to this kind of bombing in the present war, for reasons of self-interest (pp. 30, 41, 42, 47, 72, 74). England started building her strategic force in 1936 (p. 30). (Charles J. V. Murphy, "The Airmen and the Invasion," *Life*, April 10, 1944, p. 95, says the English air force "has been painstakingly assembled since 1940 to do area bombing." General Arnold says that the general plans for our present bombing of Germany were laid in the summer of 1941.) Mr. Spaight thinks that England would inevitably have gone bombing in Germany even if Germany had never bombed England (p. 149). "We began to bomb objectives on the German mainland before Germans began to bomb objectives on the British mainland. That is a historical fact which has been publicly admitted" (p. 68). But Germany was the first to bomb towns in the present war, e.g., in Norway (p. 150). Warsaw and Rotterdam were different because there the bombing was tactical—in immediate support of the invading army (p. 43, 149). Mr. Spaight's contention is that to Great Britain belongs the credit and honor of adopting long ago the strategy now being applied (pp. 73, 143). (At the Disarmament Conference of 1932, Italy proposed the abolition of the bombing airplane and was supported by Germany, Russia, and the United States. Great Britain blocked the proposal because she wanted to reserve the use of the bomber for "police work," i.e., for bombing unruly native populations in India. According to *Time*, July 7, 1943, it was Sir Arthur Harris who introduced this technique.) Mr. Spaight is in doubt as to whether the English reservation killed the 1932 proposal at Geneva, but thinks we should at least say: "They [Eden and Lord Londonderry] did not kill the proposal to abolish bombing. If they had done so they would have done something of inestimable value to our national interests and the cause of civilization."

[27]"The Non-Obliterators," *Saturday Review of Literature*, April 8, 1944, p. 14.

[28]On July 15, 1941, Churchill approved this sentiment: "We will mete out to the Germans the measure and more than the measure that they have meted

robot bombing. An editorial in the *Boston Herald* asks: "Why not go all out on bombings? . . . *Why be nice about the undefended towns and cities?* . . . The time-honored system of tit for tat is the only one which Hitler and his Germans can understand."[29] The *New York Times* had an editorial along the same lines.[30] And in a letter to that paper one Carl Beck demands an ultimatum from the chiefs of the four United Nations, threatening Germany that "for every prisoner murdered we will take ten German lives, for all civilian mass murder we will take an equivalent number of Germans the minute we reach their soil—we ourselves will treat all prisoners according to civilized warfare."[31]

Naturally one does not expect political leaders to assert definitely that they intend to kill women and children.[32] The feelings of the whole civilized world are so completely in accord with the traditional distinction between innocent and guilty, and such a very large number of people (with votes) everywhere consider themselves to be among the innocent, that it would probably be political suicide to announce explicitly such a policy; and even from the military point of view it would provide the enemy with priceless propaganda. Any attack on the innocent civil population will always be covered up by a euphemistic name, like "area" bombing, or simply written off under the general absolution of "military necessity." My point, therefore, is to indicate that we have good grounds for suspecting that the *de facto* intent of the air strategists is not governed by the morality of direct and indirect intent at all, and that it is naive and

---

out to us." He also made revengeful statements before the United States Congress regarding Japan (Vera Brittain, "Not Made in Germany," *Fellowship*, X, June 1944, p. 108). Mr. Churchill gave the Golden Rule a new twist in a speech broadcast on May 10, 1942. He said that Bomber Command had done a great thing in teaching "a race of itching warriors that there is something after all in the old and still valid Golden Rule" (Spaight, *Bombing Vindicated*, p. 103).

[29]*Boston Herald*, July 4, 1944 (italics added).

[30]*New York Times,* June 1, 1944.

[31]*New York Times*, July 20, 1944. The question of revenge does not constitute any theoretical problem for the moralist. Such a motive includes hatred and is clearly immoral. It violates the Gospel law. But reprisals, as that term is used in international law, must be distinguished from revenge. When used as a last resort and with due regard for the moral law, they can be legitimate; cf. Louis le Fur, *Précis de droit international public* (Paris: Dalloz, 1939), pp. 873, 908. But their use is always dangerous, because it leads to a grim competition of frightfulness; cf. A. Messineo, S.J., "Le rappresaglie e la guerra," *Civilta Cattolica*, Anno 92, Vol. I (March 15, 1941), p. 420.

[32]The statement of Mr. Stanley Baldwin quoted by Fr. Joseph Keating is exceptional: "The only defense is offense which means that you have to kill more women and children more quickly than the enemy [can] if you want to save yourselves" (quoted in "The Ethics of Bombing," *The Catholic Mind*, XXXVI, July 22, 1938, p. 279, note 3); the speech was made in the House of Commons on November 10, 1932.

unrealistic to imagine them conforming themselves to the principle of the double effect on this score.

The question of a proportionately grave cause   But furthermore, the question of direct or indirect intent is not decisive in the application of the principle of the double effect. There still remains the question of proportionately grave causes to justify the alleged "permission" of the evil. Even if I doubted, therefore, about the abstract possibility of "holding back the intention," I would have no doubt about the immorality of obliteration bombing. When it is carried out on the scale described, I am convinced it lacks all sufficient justification. And though the question of proportionate cause involves military considerations on which the moralist cannot speak with authority, yet it also includes strictly moral elements. And so, leaving aside for the moment the authority of the Pope (whose voice can be effectively appealed to on this question), as well as those principles of charity and humanity which, by law and example, Christ made the very groundwork of our religion, let us see whether the element of proportionate cause is satisfied in the general strategy of obliteration.

The principal reason alleged to justify the infliction of enormous agonies on hundreds of thousands and even millions of innocent persons by obliteration bombing is the reason of military necessity, or of shortening the war. We hear that "it must be done to win the war"; "it will shorten the war and save our soldiers' lives"; "it will liberate Europe and enable us to feed the starving sooner." Major General J. F. C. Fuller, writing long before obliteration bombing was an issue, said: "When however it is realized that to enforce policy, and not to kill, is the objective [in war] and that the policy of a nation though maintained and enforced by her soldiers and sailors is not fashioned by them but by the civil population, surely then if a few civilians get killed in the struggle they have nothing to complain of—'dulce et decorum est pro patria mori!' "[33] Mr. J. M. Spaight makes the amazing claim that the long-range bomber, built for operations like the present one in Germany, is the savior of lives, of civilization, and the cornerstone of future peace.

Now in the practical estimation of proportionate cause it is fundamental to recognize that an evil which is certain and extensive and immediate will rarely be compensated for by a problematical, speculative, future good. The evil wrought by obliteration is certain injury and death, here and now, to hundreds of thousands, and an

[33]Quoted by John K. Ryan, *Modern War and Basic Ethics*, p. 115, note. Dr. Ryan gives many references to writers who hold the theory that attacking civil populations is a humanizing element in war.

incalculable destruction of their property. The ultimate good which is supposed to compensate for this evil is of a very speculative character.

When Great Britain first adopted obliteration as a policy, Mr. Churchill called it an experiment. He did not know whether it would work or not.[34] The U. S. Army Air Forces in their account of the first year's work in Germany say: "*Target: Germany* is the story of an experiment," and admit that after a year "the final evaluation is yet to be made," and from the nature of the case cannot be made ahead of time or even at the time of the bombing. The effects on future battles are too far removed—sometimes not felt for six months.[35] To the question, "Will bombing win the war?", *Target: Germany* replies: "To the military logician the question is beside the point. Aerial assault is directed both at the enemy's will to resist and his means to resist. One may collapse before the other; either eventuality is desirable. Bombing will be carried out to the fullest extent in either case."[36] Naturally the authors of *Target: Germany* have confidence in the military effectiveness of their strategy, but they are far from talking in terms of certainty, and they are talking of the whole air strategy, both the British and American assignments. It is well known, besides, that many military men and many air force men doubted the effectiveness of the strategic bombing of industrial centers. The French military officials were against it.[37] According to Mr. Spaight, the Germans have never believed in its military effectiveness for Germany.[38] This is not the time when we can expect the opponents of strategic bombing to voice their views. After all they are in the service, we are at war, and the defenders of the bombing have had their ideas officially endorsed. But on the merits of the question, whether this bombing is a profitable and effective strategy from the military point of view, there is disagreement among the military experts themselves.

We are told by a competent reporter of facts that Churchill had "powerful critics of the British Bomber command inside his own Air Ministry. . . . [Certain] British airmen . . . have come to distrust his

---

[34]According to *Time*, July 7, 1943, Churchill "stated the reaction of the global strategists when he said, 'The experiment is well worth trying so long as other measures are not excluded.' " This was after Harris and Eaker had given assurances that Germany could be bombed out of the war in 1943. Seven months later this had not taken place.

[35]*Target: Germany*, p. 19.

[36]*Target: Germany*, p. 118; also p. 115; "The purpose of this book has been factually to record the testing of a new concept of vertical warfare."

[37]Spaight, *Bombing Vindicated*, pp. 70-71.

[38]*Loc. cit.* Mr. Spaight himself has no doubt about the policy.

bomber strategy. . . . The night attacks on German industrial populations, they think, are too haphazard, the targets too far back in the production sequence, to affect German military strength *now*. They argue that quite aside from ethical considerations Harris' technique . . . is not necessarily shortening the war." The same writer tells us that there is a "small but influential group of British intellectuals who have been arguing privately that the economic and social problems deriving from the wrecking of German communities will prove more disastrous in the end than the immediate problem which bombing is supposed to bypass."[39]

The United States' air leaders, though fully co-operating with British obliteration methods, cannot help betraying their preference for American precision work. And criticism of the general strategy over Germany is not unheard of among military men in this country. In a forthcoming book, Colonel W. F. Kernan, the well-known strategist, will express his opinion that bombing cities is the wrong strategy—this from a purely military point of view.[40]

It remains to be seen, therefore, whether this type of bombing is a military *necessity* in order to win the war sooner and save British and American lives. The bombing of Monte Cassino was called a military necessity in order to save American lives; but the military experts proved to be mistaken. "Military necessity" can become a mere catchword, and a cloak for every sort of excess, especially when the judgment is made entirely on military grounds without taking into account other factors, such as psychology (not to mention morality).[41] Germany's strategic bombing of England was held to be a failure partly because it stiffened the resistance of the English. Who can say to what extent our obliteration will strengthen rather than weaken the German will to resist—or to what excesses of cruel retribution against our soldiers the people will be aroused? There are many military men who still agree with Marshal Foch: "You cannot scare a great nation into submission by destroying her

[39]Charles J. V. Murphy, "The Airmen and the Invasion," *Life*, Apr. 10, 1944, p. 95.

[40]Col. Kernan is the author of *Defense Will Not Win This War* (Boston: Little, Brown, 1942), and *We Can Win This War* (Boston: Little, Brown, 1943). His forthcoming book will be called *Let's Be Heroic*, and it is in Chapter V that he expresses his views on the strategy used over Germany.

[41]Vera Brittain, "Not Made in Germany," *Fellowship*, X (June 1944), 108, answers the President's argument that bombing, in the opinion of an overwhelming percentage of military authorities, is shortening the war. She says: "It is, however, well known that most military authorities possess expert minds which are necessarily limited to their own sphere. With rare exceptions they are apt to perceive only one aspect of the present and little of the future, and their judgments tend to be based on mathematical calculations rather than on human reactions."

cities."[42] Members of the French hierarchy have warned us that our bombing in France (the argument holds a fortiori for Germany), "by striking blindly at innocent populations, by mutilating the face of our country, might engender between our nations a volume of hatred which not even the peace will be able to assuage."[43] And more than one observer has noted the extreme cautiousness with which Russia has resorted to this type of bombing, in western Europe. Russia is not making enemies unnecessarily, where she intends to govern.

The next argument—that obliteration bombing will hasten the day when our victorious arms will enable us to feed the starving millions abused by the Axis—seems to contain an element of hypocrisy. If we wanted to feed starving Europe, we (the United States and Great Britain) could feed millions of the innocent right now. Mr. Hoover has pointed out the way. It does not become us to omit to feed the millions we certainly could feed now, and adopt obliteration with its immense torture of the innocent on the plea that it *may* enable us to feed the hungry later on; especially when President Roosevelt's personal envoy, Colonel Donovan, spoke as follows to the French ambassador at Ankara in the spring of 1941: "The American people are prepared to starve every Frenchman if that's necessary to defeat Hitler."[44] It would be more forthright to argue as Mr. Spaight does, that *since* it is permissible to starve civilians, then why is it not permissible to go on bombing them?[45] At least this points up the moral issues instead of beclouding them.

To all these bizarre claims, that attacks on the civilian population are a humanizing element in modern war, I think the following words of Dr. Ryan are relevant: "From a merely utilitarian standpoint these attacks cannot be justified, for they would spread destruction rather than restrict it, lengthen a war rather than shorten it, provide bitter causes for future conflicts rather than the conditions of a lasting peace."[46]

I conclude from all this that it is illegitimate to appeal to the principle of the double effect when the alleged proportionate cause is speculative, future, and problematical, while the evil effect is definite, widespread, certain, and immediate.

But my argument can be pressed still further, and on more general grounds. Even if obliteration bombing did shorten this war (and if

---

[42]Quoted by John K. Ryan, *Modern War and Basic Ethics*, p. 117, note.

[43]*London Tablet*, CLXXXIII (May 20, 1944), p. 246.

[44]Quoted in *America*, LXX (June 10, 1944), p. 279.

[45]*Bombing Vindicated*, p. 120.

[46]*Modern War and Basic Ethics* (st. ed.; Washington, D. C., 1933), p. 101.

the war ends tomorrow we shall never know whether it was this type of bombing that ended it), and even if it did save many military lives, we still must consider *what the result for the future will be if this means of warfare is made generally legitimate.*

Can we afford to justify from this time forward obliteration bombing as a legitimate instrument of war? Once it is conceded that this is a lawful means of waging war, then it is equally available to our enemies, present and future. They will have just as much right to use it against us as they have to use guns against our soldiers. I do not believe any shortening of the present war, or any saving of the lives of our soldiers (problematical at best) is a cause sufficient to justify on moral grounds the use of obliteration bombing in the future.

For in practice, though one may adhere verbally to the distinction between innocent and guilty, the obliteration of great sections of cities, including whole districts of workers' residences, means the abandonment of that distinction as an effective moral norm. When the innocent civil population can be wiped out on such a large scale very little is left practically of the rights of the innocent. Each new and more terrifying procedure, with more and more loss of innocent life, can always be defended as a mere extension of the principle, justified by the desperate military necessities of the case. The wiping out of whole cities is a reversion to barbarism as far as civilian rights are concerned. Already there is talk of using gas when we go into the Far East. The present demands of legislators, editors, and others for the indiscriminate bombing of *non-industrial* towns in Germany is a clear example of an inevitable tendency—once you get used to the idea of obliteration, and justify it.

This is another way of saying that the recognition of obliteration bombing will easily and quickly lead to the recognition of total war itself. Some may say, of course, that we recognize total war already and are waging it. But that would be a gross exaggeration. Dr. Guido Gonella tells us: "The totality of war is generally understood in a three-fold sense. It applies to the *persons* by whom and against whom warlike action is exercised, to the *means* which are employed in war, and to the *places* where warlike action takes place. (The term war-like action is taken in the broadest sense, including not only military action but also every form of manifestation of hostility, for example, by economic blockade, by the war of nerves etc. . . .)" And again: "If total war is defended as a war which is fought without regard to any limitations affecting persons, or means of warfare, or places," then it must be condemned as immoral.[47] All Catholics,

[47]*A World to Reconstruct*, Chap. XII.

following the lead of the Pope, the hierarchy, and firmly established moral principles, condemn total war in this, its fullest, sense. To say that war need know no restraint in these matters is equivalent to asserting that men at war are no longer bound by the natural law at all. And so the elimination of total war was one of the main objectives of the Holy Father's Christmas message of 1941.

I do not think any American or British statesman or leader believes we are waging, or should wage war in this utterly unrestrained and barbaric manner. But I do think the theory of total war, proclaimed unashamedly by some of our enemies, has made an impression on leaders and on the popular mind. The phrase has been tossed about like the phrase "military necessity," and it becomes a cover-all to hide and excuse practices which would otherwise be readily recognized as immoral. The false notion that today whole peoples are waging war against whole peoples is insinuated or openly propagated, and the conclusion is drawn that whole peoples are legitimate objects of attack.[48]

Now the air bombardment of civilian centers is a symbol of total war in its worst sense. It is the first thing that comes to mind when the phrase "total war" is heard. The air bombardment of great centers of population lets down the bars, and opens up enormous categories of persons, hitherto immune, against whom warlike action can now be taken; it changes the scene of war like activity from the battlefield to the city, and not only to the war factories but to the residential districts of the workers; and it uses explosives and incendiaries to a hitherto unheard of degree, leaving only one more step to go to the use of poison gas or bacteriological war. This means that obliteration bombing has taken us a long step in the direction of immoral total war. To justify it, will, I believe, make it exceedingly difficult to draw the line at further barbarities in practice. If the leaders of the world were well educated in moral matters and conscientious in the application of Christian moral principles to the waging of war, the danger might not be so real. But half of them are not Christian at all and worship material force as an ultimate, while almost all of them are immersed in a completely secularized tradition. If *moralists* grant them the vast horrors of obliteration

---

[48]See S.L.A. Marshall, *Blitzkrieg* (New York: William Morrow, 1940), especially pp. 32, 111, 145, 149; George Fielding Eliot, *Bombs Bursting in Air* (New York: Reynal and Hitchcock, 1939), pp. 23-25; Lt. Col. Harold E. Hartney, *What the Citizen Should Know about the Air Forces* (New York: Norton, 1942), p. 205; Fletcher Pratt, *America and Total War* (New York: Smith and Durell, 1941); Cyril Falls, *The Nature of Modern Warfare* (New York: Oxford University Press, 1941); E.J. Kingston-McCloughry, *Winged Warfare* (London: Jonathan Cape, 1937); General Wladyslaw Sikorski, *Modern Warfare* (New York: Roy Publishers, 1943); Giulio Douhet, *The Command of the Air* (New York: Coward McCann, 1942).

bombing, what will stop them from that point on? If one were merely applying the principle of the double effect to the act of an individual bombardier dropping a bomb, such considerations would not be very much to the point; but when the question is the whole strategy of obliteration, these larger considerations, the thought of future consequences for the whole civilized world, are the most important elements to be remembered in estimating proportionate cause. . . .

Elizabeth Anscombe
War and Murder

The Use of Violence by Rulers

42 Since there are always thieves and frauds and men who commit violent attacks on their neighbours and murderers, and since without law backed by adequate force there are usually gangs of bandits; and since there are in most places laws administered by people who command violence to enforce the laws against law-breakers; the question arises: what is a just attitude to this exercise of violent coercive power on the part of rulers and their subordinate officers?

Two attitudes are possible: one, that the world is an absolute jungle and that the exercise of coercive power by rulers is only a manifestation of this; and the other, that it is both necessary and right that there should be this exercise of power, that through it the world is much less of a jungle than it could possibly be without it, so that one should in principle be glad of the existence of such power, and only take exception to its unjust exercise.

It is so clear that the world is less of a jungle because of rulers and laws, and that the exercise of coercive power is essential to these institutions as they are now—all this is so obvious, that probably only Tennysonian conceptions of progress enable people who do not wish to separate themselves from the world to think that nevertheless such violence is objectionable, that some day, in this present dispensation, we shall do without it, and that the pacifist is the man who sees and tries to follow the ideal course, which future civilization must one day pursue. It is an illusion, which would be fantastic if it were not so familiar.

Elizabeth Anscombe is a professor of philosophy at Cambridge University and was formerly a Fellow at Somerville College, Oxford. Among her major philosophical contributions are *Intentions* (1957), *An Introduction to Wittgenstein's Tractatus* (1959), and *Three Philosophers* (with Peter Geach, 1961).
Her essay "War and Murder" first appeared in a collection of essays written by five British academicians, all of whom were Catholic and all of whom were concerned about the problems of nuclear warfare. It is reprinted here from *Nuclear Weapons: A Catholic Response,* edited by Walter Stein, pp. 45-62. Copyright © 1961 by the Merlin Press Ltd., published by Sheed and Ward Inc., New York. It appears with the permission of the author and the publishers.

In a peaceful and law abiding country such as England, it may not be immediately obvious that the rulers need to command violence to the point of fighting to the death those that would oppose it; but brief reflection shews that this is so. For those who oppose the force that backs law will not always stop short of fighting to the death and cannot always be put down short of fighting to the death.

Then only if it is in itself evil violently to coerce resistant wills, can the exercise of coercive power by rulers be bad as such. Against such a conception, if it were true, the necessity and advantage of the exercise of such power would indeed be a useless plea. But that conception is one that makes no sense unless it is accompanied by a theory of withdrawal from the world as man's only salvation; and it is in any case a false one. We are taught that God retains the evil will of the devil within limits by violence: we are not given a picture of God permitting to the devil all that he is capable of. There is current a conception of Christianity as having revealed that the defeat of evil must always be by pure love without coercion; this at least is shewn to be false by the foregoing consideration. And without the alleged revelation there could be no reason to believe such a thing.

To think that society's coercive authority is evil is akin to thinking the flesh evil and family life evil. These things belong to the present constitution of mankind; and if the exercise of coercive power is a manifestation of evil, and not the just means of restraining it, then human nature is totally depraved in a manner never taught by Christianity. For society is essential to human good; and society without coercive power is generally impossible.

The same authority which puts down internal dissension, which promulgates laws and restrains those who break them if it can, must equally oppose external enemies. These do not merely comprise those who attack the borders of the people ruled by the authority; but also, for example, pirates and desert bandits, and, generally, those beyond the confines of the country ruled whose activities are viciously harmful to it. The Romans, once their rule in Gaul was established, were eminently justified in attacking Britain, where were nurtured the Druids whose pupils infested northern Gaul and whose practices struck the Romans themselves as "dira immanitas." Further, there being such a thing as the common good of mankind, and visible criminality against it, how can we doubt the excellence of such a proceeding as that violent suppression of the man-stealing business[1] which the British government took it into its head to engage in under Palmerston? The present-day conception of

---

[1] It is ignorance to suppose that it takes modern liberalism to hate and condemn this. It is cursed and subject to the death penalty in the Mosaic law. Under that code, too, runaway slaves of all nations had asylum in Israel.

"aggression," like so many strongly influential conceptions, is a bad one. Why *must* it be wrong to strike the first blow in a struggle? The only question is, who is in the right.

Here, however, human pride, malice and cruelty are so usual that it is true to say that wars have mostly been mere wickedness on both sides. Just as an individual will constantly think himself in the right, whatever he does, and yet there is still such a thing as being in the right, so nations will constantly wrongly think themselves to be in the right—and yet there is still such a thing as their being in the right. Palmerston doubtless had no doubts in prosecuting the opium war against China, which was diabolical; just as he exulted in putting down the slavers. But there is no question but that he was a monster in the one thing, and a just man in the other.

The probability is that warfare is injustice, that a life of military service is a bad life "militia or rather malitia," as St. Anselm called it. This probability is greater than the probability (which also exists) that membership of a police force will involve malice, because of the character of warfare: the extraordinary occasions it offers for viciously unjust proceedings on the part of military commanders and warring governments, which at the time attract praise and not blame from their people. It is equally the case that the life of a ruler is usually a vicious life: but that does not shew that ruling is as such a vicious activity.

The principal wickedness which is a temptation to those engaged in warfare is the killing of the innocent, which may often be done with impunity and even to the glory of those who do it. In many places and times it has been taken for granted as a natural part of waging war: the commander, and especially the conqueror, massacres people by the thousand, either because this is part of his glory, or as a terrorizing measure, or as part of his tactics.

Innocence and the Right to Kill
Intentionally

It is necessary to dwell on the notion of non-innocence here employed. Innocence is a legal notion; but here, the accused is not pronounced guilty under an existing code of law, under which he has been tried by an impartial judge, and therefore made the target of attack. There is hardly a possibility of this; for the administration of justice is something that takes place under the aegis of a sovereign authority; but in warfare—or the putting down by violence of civil disturbance—the sovereign authority is itself engaged as a party to the dispute and is not subject to a further earthly and temporal authority which can judge the issue and pronounce against the accused. The stabler the society, the rarer it will be for the sovereign authority to have to do anything but apprehend its internal enemy and have him tried: but even in the stablest society there are occasions when the authority has to fight its internal enemy to the point of killing, as happens in the struggle with external belligerent forces in international warfare; and then the characterization of its enemy as non-innocent has not been ratified by legal process.

This, however, does not mean that the notion of innocence fails in this situation. What is required, for the people attacked to be non-innocent in the relevant sense, is that they should themselves be engaged in an objectively unjust proceeding which the attacker has the right to make his concern; or—the commonest case—should be unjustly attacking him. Then he can attack them with a view to stopping them; and also their supply lines and armament factories. But people whose mere existence and activity supporting existence by growing crops, making clothes, etc. constitute an impediment to him—such people are innocent and it is murderous to attack them, or make them a target for an attack which he judges will help him towards victory. For murder is the deliberate killing of the innocent, whether for its own sake or as a means to some further end.

The right to attack with a view to killing is something that belongs only to rulers and those whom they command to do it. I have argued that it does belong to rulers precisely because of that threat of violent coercion exercised by those in authority which is essential to the existence of human societies. It ought not to be pretended that rulers and their subordinates do not choose[2] the killing of their enemies as a means, when it has come to fighting in which they are determined to win and their enemies resist to the point of killing: this holds even in internal disturbances.

When a private man struggles with an enemy he has no right to aim to kill him, unless in the circumstances of the attack on him he can be considered as endowed with the authority of the law and the struggle comes to that point. By a "private" man, I mean a man in a society; I am not speaking of men on their own, without government, in remote places; for such men are neither public servants nor "private." The plea of self-defence (or the defence of someone else) made by a private man who has killed someone else must in conscience—even if not in law—be a plea that the death of the other was not intended, but was a side effect of the measures taken to ward off the attack. To shoot to kill, to set lethal man-traps, or, say, to lay poison for someone from whom one's life

[2]The idea that they may lawfully do what they do, but should not *intend* the death of those they attack, has been put forward and, when suitably expressed, may seem high-minded. But someone who can fool himself into this twist of thought will fool himself into justifying anything, however atrocious, by means of it.

is in danger, are forbidden. The deliberate choice of inflicting death in a struggle is the right only of ruling authorities and their subordinates.

In saying that a private man may not choose to kill, we are touching on the principle of "double effect." The denial of this has been the corruption of non-Catholic thought, and its abuse the corruption of Catholic thought. Both have disastrous consequences which we shall see. This principle is not accepted in English law: the law is said to allow no distinction between the foreseen and the intended consequences of an action. Thus, if I push a man over a cliff when he is menacing my life, his death is considered as intended by me, but the intention to be justifiable for the sake of self-defence. Yet the lawyers would hardly find the laying of poison tolerable as an act of self-defence, but only killing by a violent action in a moment of violence. Christian moral theologians have taught that even here one may not seek the death of the assailant, but may in default of other ways of self-defence use such violence as will in fact result in his death. The distinction is evidently a fine one in some cases: what, it may be asked, can the intention be, if it can be said to be absent in this case, except a mere wish or desire?

And yet in other cases the distinction is very clear. If I go to prison rather than perform some action, no reasonable person will call the incidental consequences of my refusal—the loss of my job, for example—intentional just because I knew they must happen. And in the case of the administration of a pain-relieving drug in mortal illness, where the doctor knows the drug may very well kill the patient if the illness does not do so first, the distinction is evident; the lack of it has led an English judge to talk nonsense about the administration of the drug's not having *really* been the cause of death in such a case, even though a post mortem shews it was. For everyone understands that it is a very different thing so to administer a drug, and to administer it with the intention of killing. However, the principle of double effect has more important applications in warfare, and I shall return to it later.

The Influence of Pacifism

Pacifism has existed as a considerable movement in English speaking countries ever since the first world war. I take the doctrine of pacifism to be that it is *eo ipso* wrong to fight in wars, not the doctrine that it is wrong to be compelled to, or that any man, or some men, may refuse; and I think it false for the reasons that I have given. But I now want to consider the very remarkable effects it has had: for I believe its influence to have been enormous, far exceeding its influence on its own adherents.

We should note first that pacifism has as its background conscription and enforced military service for all men. Without conscription, pacifism is a private opinion that will keep those who hold it out of armies, which they are in any case not obliged to join. Now universal conscription, except for the most extraordinary reasons, i.e. as a regular habit among most nations, is such a horrid evil that the refusal of it automatically commands a certain amount of respect and sympathy.

We are not here concerned with the pacifism of some peculiar sect which in any case draws apart from the world to a certain extent, but with a pacifism of people in the world, who do not want to be withdrawn from it. For some of these, pacifism is prevented from being a merely theoretical attitude because they are liable to, and so are prepared to resist conscription; or are able directly to effect the attitude of some who are so liable.

A powerful ingredient in this pacifism is the prevailing image of Christianity. This image commands a sentimental respect among people who have no belief in Christianity, that is to say, in Christian dogmas; yet do have a certain belief in an ideal which they conceive to be part of "true Christianity." It is therefore important to understand this image of Christianity and to know how false it is. Such understanding is relevant, not merely to those who wish to believe Christianity, but to all who, without the least wish to believe, are yet profoundly influenced by this image of it.

According to this image, Christianity is an ideal and beautiful religion, impracticable except for a few rare characters. It preaches a God of love whom there is no reason to fear; it marks an escape from the conception presented in the Old Testament, of a vindictive and jealous God who will terribly punish his enemies. The "Christian" God is a *roi fainéant*, whose only triumph is in the Cross; his appeal is to goodness and unselfishness, and to follow him is to act according to the Sermon on the Mount—to turn the other cheek and to offer no resistance to evil. In this account some of the evangelical counsels are chosen as containing the whole of Christian ethics: that is, they are made into precepts. (Only some of them; it is not likely that someone who deduces the *duty* of pacifism from the Sermon on the Mount and the rebuke to Peter, will agree to take "Give to him that asks of you" equally as a universally binding precept.)

The turning of counsels into precepts results in high-sounding principles. Principles that are mistakenly high and strict are a trap; they may easily lead in the end directly or indirectly to the justification of monstrous things. Thus if the evangelical counsel about poverty were turned into a precept forbidding property owning, people would pay lip service to it as the ideal, while in practice they went in for swindling. "Absolute honesty!" it would be said: "I can respect that—but of course that means having no property; and while I respect those who follow that course, I have to compromise with the sordid world myself." If then one must "compromise with evil" by owning property and engaging in trade, then the amount of swindling one does will depend on convenience. This imaginary case is paralleled by what is so commonly said: absolute pacifism is an ideal; unable to follow that, and committed to "compromise with evil," one must go the whole hog and wage war à outrance.

The truth about Christianity is that it is a severe and practicable religion, not a beautifully ideal but impracticable one. Its moral precepts, (except for the stricter laws about marriage that Christ enacted, abrogating some of the permissions of the Old Law) are those of the Old Testament; and its God is the God of Israel.

It is ignorance of the New Testament that hides this from people. It is characteristic of pacifism to denigrate the Old Testament and exalt the New: something quite contrary to the teaching of the New Testament itself, which always looks back to and leans upon the Old. How typical it is that the words of Christ "You have heard it said, an eye for an eye and a tooth for a tooth, but I say to you . . ." are taken as a repudiation of the ethic of the Old Testament! People seldom look up the occurrence of this phrase in the juridical code of the Old Testament, where it belongs, and is the admirable principle of law for the punishment of certain crimes, such as procuring the wrongful punishment of another by perjury. People often enough now cite the phrase to justify private revenge; no doubt this was as often "heard said" when Christ spoke of it. But no justification for this exists in the personal ethic taught by the Old Testament. On the contrary. What do we find? "Seek no revenge," (Leviticus xix, 18), and "If you find your enemy's ox or ass going astray, take it back to him; if you see the ass of someone who hates you lying under his burden, and would forbear to help him; you must help him" (Exodus xxiii, 4-5). And "If your enemy is hungry, give him food, if thirsty, give him drink" (Proverbs xxv, 21).

This is only one example; given space, it would be easy to shew how false is the conception of Christ's teaching as *correcting* the religion of the ancient Israelites, and substituting a higher and more "spiritual" religion for theirs. Now the false picture I have described plays an important part in the pacifist ethic and in the ethic of the many people who are not pacifists but are influenced by pacifism.

To extract a pacifist doctrine—i.e. a condemnation of the use of force by the ruling authorities, and of soldiering as a profession—from the evangelical counsels and the rebuke to Peter, is to disregard what else is in the New Testament. It is to forget St. John's direction to soldiers: "do not blackmail people; be content with your pay"; and Christ's commendation of the centurion, who compared his authority over his men to Christ's. On a pacifist view, this must be much as if a madam in a brothel had said: "I know what authority is, I tell this girl to do this, and she does it . . ." and Christ had commended her faith. A centurion was the first Gentile to be baptized; there is no suggestion in the New Testament that soldiering was regarded as incompatible with Christianity. The martyrology contains many names of soldiers whose occasion for martyrdom was not any objection to soldiering, but a refusal to perform idolatrous acts.

Now, it is one of the most vehement and repeated teachings of the Judaeo-Christian tradition that the shedding of innocent blood is forbidden by the divine law. No man may be punished except for his own crime, and those "whose feet are swift to shed innocent blood" are always represented as God's enemies.

For a long time the main outlines of this teaching have seemed to be merely obvious morality: hence, for example, I have read a passage by Ronald Knox complaining of the "endless moralizing," interspersed in records of meanness, cowardice, spite, cruelty, treachery and murder, which forms so much of the Old Testament. And indeed, that it is terrible to kill the innocent is very obvious; the morality that so stringently forbids it must make a great appeal to mankind, especially to the poor threatened victims. Why should it need the thunder of Sinai and the suffering and preaching of the prophets to promulgate such a law? But human pride and malice are everywhere so strong that now, with the fading of Christianity from the mind of the West, this morality once more stands out as a demand which strikes pride- and fear-ridden people as too intransigent. For Knox, it seemed so obvious as to be dull; and he failed to recognize the bloody and beastly records that it accompanies for the dry truthfulness about human beings that so characterizes the Old Testament.[3]

Now pacifism teaches people to make no distinction between the shedding of innocent blood and the shedding of any human blood. And in this way pacifism has corrupted enormous numbers of people who will not act according to its tenets. They become convinced that a number of things are wicked which are not; hence, seeing no way of avoiding "wickedness," they set no limits to it. How endlessly pacifists argue that all war must be *à outrance*! that those

---

[3]It is perhaps necessary to remark that I am not here adverting to the total extermination of certain named tribes of Canaan that is said by the Old Testament to have been commanded by God. That is something quite outside the provisions of the Mosaic Law for dealings in war.

who wage war must go as far as technological advance permits in the destruction of the enemy's people. As if the Napoleonic wars were perforce fuller of massacres than the French war of Henry V of England. It is not true: the reverse took place. Nor is technological advance particularly relevant; it is mere squeamishness that deters people who would consent to area bombing from the enormous massacres *by hand* that used once to be committed.

The policy of obliterating cities was adopted by the Allies in the last war; they need not have taken that step, and it was taken largely out of a villainous hatred, and as corollary to the policy, now universally denigrated, of seeking "unconditional surrender." (That policy itself was visibly wicked, and could be and was judged so at the time; it is not surprising that it led to disastrous consequences, even if no one was clever and detached enough to foresee this at the time.)

Pacifism and the respect for pacifism is not the only thing that has led to a universal forgetfulness of the law against killing the innocent; but it has had a great share in it.

The Principle of Double Effect

Catholics, however, can hardly avoid paying at least lip-service to that law. So we must ask: how is it that there has been so comparatively little conscience exercised on the subject among them? The answer is: double-think about double effect.

The distinction between the intended, and the merely foreseen, effects of a voluntary action is indeed absolutely essential to Christian ethics. For Christianity forbids a number of things as being bad in themselves. But if I am answerable for the foreseen consequences of an action or refusal, as much as for the action itself, then these prohibitions will break down. If someone innocent will die unless I do a wicked thing, then on this view I am his murderer in refusing: so all that is left to me is to weigh up evils. Here the theologian steps in with the principle of double effect and says: "No, you are no murderer, if the man's death was neither your aim nor your chosen means, and if you had to act in the way that led to it or else do something absolutely forbidden." Without understanding of this principle, anything can be—and is wont to be—justified, and the Christian teaching that in no circumstances may one commit murder, adultery, apostasy (to give a few examples) goes by the board. These absolute prohibitions of Christianity by no means exhaust its ethic; there is a large area where what is just is determined partly by a prudent weighing up of consequences. But the prohibitions are bedrock, and without them the Christian ethic goes to pieces. Hence the necessity of the notion of double effect.

At the same time, the principle has been repeatedly abused from the seventeenth century up till now. The causes lie in the history of philosophy. From the seventeenth century till now what may be called Cartesian psychology has dominated the thought of philosophers and theologians. According to this psychology, an intention was an interior act of the mind which could be produced at will. Now if intention is all important—as it is—in determining the goodness or badness of an action, then, on this theory of what intention is, a marvellous way offered itself of making any action lawful. You only had to "direct your intention" in a suitable way. In practice, this means making a little speech to yourself: "What I mean to be doing is. . . ."

This perverse doctrine has occasioned repeated condemnations by the Holy See from the seventeenth century to the present day. Some examples will suffice to shew how the thing goes. Typical doctrines from the seventeenth century were that it is all right for a servant to hold the ladder for his criminous master so long as he is merely avoiding the sack by doing so; or that a man might wish for and rejoice at his parent's death so long as what he had in mind was the gain to himself; or that it is not simony to offer money, not *as a price* for the spiritual benefit, but only *as an inducement* to give it. A condemned doctrine from the present day is that the practice of *coitus reservatus* is permissible: such a doctrine could only arise in connexion with that "direction of intention" which sets everything right no matter what one does. A man makes a practice of withdrawing, telling himself that he *intends* not to ejaculate; of course (if that is his practice) he usually does so, but then the event is "accidental" and *praeter intentionem*: it is, in short, a case of "double effect."

This same doctrine is used to prevent any doubts about the obliteration bombing of a city. The devout Catholic bomber secures by a "direction of intention" that any shedding of innocent blood that occurs is "accidental." I know a Catholic boy who was puzzled at being told by his schoolmaster that it was an *accident* that the people of Hiroshima and Nagasaki were there to be killed; in fact, however absurd it seems, such thoughts are common among priests who know that they are forbidden by the divine law to justify the direct killing of the innocent.

It is nonsense to pretend that you do not intend to do what is the means you take to your chosen end. Otherwise there is absolutely no substance to the Pauline teaching that we may not do evil that good may come.

There are a number of sophistical arguments, often or sometimes used on these topics, which need answering.

Where do you draw the line? As Dr. Johnson said, the fact of twilight does not mean you cannot tell day from night. There are borderline cases, where it is difficult to distinguish, in what is done, between means and what is incidental to, yet in the circumstances inseparable from, those means. The obliteration bombing of a city is not a borderline case.

The old "conditions for a just war" are irrelevant to the conditions of modern warfare, so that must be condemned out of hand. People who say this always envisage only major wars between the Great Powers, which Powers are indeed now "in blood stepp'd in so far" that it is unimaginable for there to be a war between them which is not a set of enormous massacres of civil populations. But these are not the only wars. Why is Finland so far free? At least partly because of the "posture of military preparedness" which, considering the character of the country, would have made subjugating the Finns a difficult and unrewarding task. The offensive of the Israelis against the Egyptians in 1956 involved no plan of making civil populations the target of military attack.

In a modern war the distinction between combatants and non-combatants is meaningless, so an attack on anyone on the enemy side is justified. This is pure nonsense; even in war, a very large number of the enemy population are just engaged in maintaining the life of the country, or are sick, or aged, or children.

It must be legitimate to maintain an opinion—viz. that the destruction of cities by bombing is lawful—if this is argued by competent theologians and the Holy See has not pronounced. The argument from the silence of the Holy See has itself been condemned by the Holy See (Denzinger, 28th Edition, 1127). How could this be a sane doctrine in view of the endless twistiness of the human mind?

Whether a war is just or not is not for the private man to judge: he must obey his government. Sometimes, this may be, especially as far as concerns causes of war. But the individual who joins in destroying a city, like a Nazi massacring the inhabitants of a village, is too obviously marked out as an enemy of the human race, to shelter behind such a plea.

Finally, horrible as it is to have to notice this, we must notice that even the arguments about double effect—which at least show that a man is not willing openly to justify the killing of the innocent—are now beginning to look old-fashioned. Some Catholics are not scrupling to say that *anything* is justified in defence of the continued existence and liberty of the Church in the West. A terrible fear of communism drives people to say this sort of thing. "Our Lord told us to fear those who can destroy body and soul, not to fear the destruction of the body" was blasphemously said to a friend of mine; meaning: "so, we must fear Russian domination more than the destruction of people's bodies by obliteration bombing."

But whom did Our Lord tell us to fear, when he said: "I will tell you whom you shall fear" and "Fear not them that can destroy the body, but fear him who can destroy body and soul in hell"? He told us to fear God the Father, who can and will destroy the unrepentant disobedient, body and soul, in hell.

A Catholic who is tempted to think on the lines I have described should remember that the Church is the spiritual Israel: that is, that Catholics are what the ancient Jews were, salt for the earth and the people of God—and that what was true of some devout Jews of ancient times can equally well be true of us now: "You compass land and sea to make a convert, and when you have done so, you make him twice as much a child of hell as yourselves." Do Catholics sometimes think that they are immune from such a possibility? That the Pharisees—who sat in the seat of Moses and who were so zealous for the true religion—were bad in ways in which we cannot be bad if we are zealous? I believe they do. But our faith teaches no such immunity, it teaches the opposite. "We are in danger all our lives long." So we have to fear God and keep his commandments, and calculate what is for the best only within the limits of that obedience, knowing that the future is in God's power and that no one can snatch away those whom the Father has given to Christ.

It is not a vague faith in the triumph of "the spirit" over force (there is little enough warrant for that), but a definite faith in the divine promises, that makes us believe that the Church cannot fail. Those, therefore, who think they must be prepared to wage a war with Russia involving the deliberate massacre of cities, must be prepared to say to God: "We had to break your law, lest your Church fail. We could not obey your commandments, for we did not believe your promises."

Michael Walzer
Moral Judgment in Time of War

When you resorted to force as the arbiter of human difficulty, you didn't know where you were going. . . . If you got deeper and deeper, there was just no limit except what was imposed by the limitations of force itself. (Dwight Eisenhower, at a press conference, January 12, 1955)

I have said to these young men that they make too much of American brutality. The Viet Cong is equally brutal. Whether one is among the battling Pakistanis and Indians, or in Watts, or in warfare anywhere, the law of violence is such that each side becomes equally vicious. To try to distinguish which is more vicious is to fail to recognize the logic of war. (Bayard Rustin, in Civil Disobedience, *an occasional paper of the Center for the Study of Democratic Institutions, 1966)*

From opposite sides of the spectrum of American politics, Eisenhower and Rustin suggest the same general theory of moral judgment in wartime. They both suggest that only one judgment is possible. War itself (Rustin is a pacifist), or some particular war, can be called just or unjust. But apparently nothing whatsoever can be said about morality *in* war, about justice or injustice in the midst of the strife, because the "logic of war" imposes brutality equally on all participants. Once war begins, there are no moral limits, only practical ones, only the "limitations of force itself" and of the "law of violence." This is a very common American view and one sufficiently serious to warrant careful refutation. I want to argue that it is profoundly wrong and that what the old lawyers called *jus in bello* (justice in war) is at least as important as *jus ad bellum* (the justice of war). War is indeed ugly, but there are degrees of ugliness and humane men must, as always, be concerned with degrees. As we

Michael Walzer is an associate professor of government at Harvard University. He is the author of a number of articles in the field of political and social philosophy and of *The Revolution of the Saints: A Study in the Origins of Radical Politics* (1965).

This essay appeared in *Dissent,* Vol. 14, No. 3 (1967), pp. 284-292. It is reprinted here with the permission of the author and *Dissent.*

watch the continued escalation of the war in Vietnam, this truth is driven home with especial force. Surely there is a point at which the means employed for the sake of this or that political goal come into conflict with a more general human purpose: the maintenance of moral standards and the survival of some sort of international society. At that point, political arguments against the use of such means are overshadowed, or ought to be, by moral arguments. At that point, war is not merely ugly, but criminal.

There are limits to what can be done in wartime, even by men convinced that they are pursuing justice. These limits are never easy to specify, and it may be that they need to be newly specified for every war. It may be that morality in war is a discretionary morality. But that does not absolve us from making judgments. It only requires that we be undogmatic, pay close attention to the facts, and struggle to grasp, as best we can, the anguish of each concrete decision.

There is an immediate improbability about Rustin's statement which is worth noting at the outset. If brutality is something that can be measured and apportioned, as he seems to suggest, then there are an infinite number of possible apportionments, and it is extremely unlikely that equality will ever be attained. In every war, the likelihood is that one side is more brutal than the other, though often the differences are too small to matter much, even to the most scrupulous of moralists. But in the case of Vietnam, where the destructive powers of the two protagonists are so radically unequal, a casual insistence on equal brutality cannot satisfy even the least scrupulous of moralists.

But perhaps what Rustin means is that each side is as brutal as it can be, given its relative power. Brutality stops only when force is limited or when it encounters superior force. That is presumably also Eisenhower's meaning. But then what the two men are talking about is, so to speak, the logic of intentions and not of behavior. Even here, however, they are probably not right. In many wars it is possible to say that different degrees of brutality are intended by the different sides. Sometimes these different intentions are an inherent part of different strategies, sometimes of different military situations. It is fairly obvious, for example, that armies fighting in friendly territory are likely to intend less brutality—whatever the limits of their power—than armies fighting amidst a hostile population. Insofar as wars are territorially limited (most wars are), one side probably has to be more brutal than the other. There are moral as well as strategic disadvantages to fighting wars in other peoples' countries.

Even if there is an identity of brutal intentions, however, it does not follow that the judgments we make of the two sides should be the same. Military decisions are guided by a kind of reciprocity: one side must do, or thinks it must do, whatever the other side does. In every war, however, there exist agreements, mostly informal, which rule out certain actions. Such agreements are usually enforced by mutual deterrence, though self-restraint also plays a part. Sometimes mutual deterrence doesn't work; perhaps one side is so strong that it need not fear retaliation from the other, whatever it does. Then self-restraint may break down also, and the agreements will be violated. After all, it might be said, the purpose of soldiers is to escape reciprocity, to inflict more damage on the enemy than he can inflict on them. Soldiers can never be blamed for taking advantage of superior strength. But that is not so, for there are many different ways of taking advantage of one's strength. In every case where superiority is attained and the war escalated beyond some previously established set of limits, a hard judgment has to be made. If the escalation breaks down limits useful not merely to the enemy, but to humanity generally, if precedents are established which make it likely that future wars will be more brutal than they would otherwise be, the initiating party can and must be condemned. This is so even if it can plausibly be said (for it can always be *said*) that the other side would have done the same if it could. Men are guilty of the crimes they commit, not the ones they are said to have wished to commit.

When we speak of brutality in wartime, we do not usually mean the killing of enemy combatants. So long as the fighting is actually in progress, virtually anything can be done to combatants—within limits set by such conventions as the ban on the use of poison gas. They have every reason to expect the worst and presumably are trained to defend themselves. It is their business to kill others until they are themselves killed. That is a brutal business when compared to peacetime pursuits; nevertheless, it involves behavior which is appropriate in time of war. Brutality most often begins with the killing of prisoners and non-combatants.

In the case of prisoners, the line between legitimate and illegitimate behavior is fairly easy to draw, in part because the condition which makes a man a prisoner is fairly easy to specify. A prisoner is an ex-combatant, helplessly in the hands of his enemies. He is entitled (according to explicit international agreements) to benevolent quarantine for the duration of the war. There has been a tendency in recent years to deny the quarantine and maintain a state of warfare, a struggle for the minds of the prisoners, even in the prison camps themselves. This is indeed a struggle limited only by the nature of available force: confessions and conversions cannot be won by killing prisoners. Virtually every form of violence short of murder, however, has been used. (See "The Destruction of Conscience in Vietnam" by Marshall Sahlins, *Dissent*, January-February 1966, for a description of ideological warfare against Vietcong prisoners; the theories behind this warfare and the methods employed in it seem to have been adapted from the Chinese Communists.) All this is criminal brutality. There is surely nothing in the "logic of war" that requires it.

With regard to non-combatants, the theoretical problems are much more difficult. This is so for a great number of reasons, several of which have been brought forward in recent months as justifications for American actions in Vietnam. First of all, modern military technology makes it very difficult to limit the damage one inflicts to enemy soldiers alone or even military installations. Even if a decision is made not to wage a full-scale campaign of terror against civilian populations, civilians are bound to be hurt and killed by what are called necessary efforts to prevent the production and transportation of military supplies. The function of the word "necessary" in arguments of this sort is worth examining. It serves to foreclose the very possibility of moral protest. Bombing is legitimate in war, the argument goes, whenever it is necessary to victory (or stalemate, or attrition, or whatever purpose is being pursued). Military necessity cannot justify wanton destruction; at the same time, moral principles cannot invalidate necessary destruction. In effect, necessity is the only standard, and the trained officers and strategists of the armed forces are the only competent judges. They solemnly conclude that civilian deaths are part of the inevitable ugliness of war.

They are sometimes right; but the argument does not hold in every case. It does not hold, for example, against all efforts to limit the geographic areas within which military judgments can apply. Rearward areas are not always subject to the same political jurisdiction as are the armies at the front. In the past, serious attempts have been made to recognize different degrees of neutrality for such areas and to admit the possibility of benevolent neutrality short of war—the kind of position the U.S. adopted vis-a-vis Great Britain in 1940 and 1941. We would have said at the time that despite the supplies we were providing for the British, German bombing of American factories would not have been morally justified (that is, it would have constituted aggression). The same principle applies with even greater force, I should think, to "little wars" where limitation of the struggle is much more likely than in big ones. Thus the U.S. participated informally in efforts to prevent the French from bombing Morocco and Tunisia during the Algerian war (February 1958), despite the constructions which French

strategists, perhaps quite reasonably, put upon the notion of military
necessity. Limits of this sort are very precarious and need to be
re-examined in every case. Exceptions are always possible. Allowance might be made for the interdiction of supplies, for example, if
it could be carried out with sufficient precision or at the very
borders of the battle area. And, of course, a point may be reached
when assistance from some ostensibly neutral country passes over
into active participation: then the limits have been broken by the
other side, and the soldiers must do what they can. Until then,
however, decisions are moral and political as well as military, and all
of us are involved.

In one sense, however, that is always true, for there are limits to
the arguments that can be made from military necessity even after
the disappearance of every distinction between battleground and
hinterland. The distinction between civilian and soldier still stands,
and among civilians that between partial participants in the business
of war (workers in munitions factories) and virtual non-participants.
In the past, systematic terror bombing of urban residential areas has
been defended in the name of military necessity—and it has been
carried out, as it probably will be again, even when the defense was
none too good. But I find it very difficult even to conceive of
circumstances in which such a defense could be good enough to
warrant the denial and eradication of these distinctions. For the bar
against the systematic slaughter of civilians is of such immense
benefit to mankind that it could only be broken by a country
absolutely certain not only that the immediate gains would be
enormous, but that the shattered limit would never again be of any
use. That is why wars to end war (or to end aggression, subversion,
or anything else) are potentially so much more brutal than wars
fought for realistic and limited objectives. They encourage men to
think that *this time anything goes*, for there will never be another
time. But there is always another time, and so *jus in bello* is always
of crucial importance.

The second argument currently being made relies on the character
of guerrilla warfare. By the special use they make of the civilian
population, it is said, the guerrillas themselves destroy all conventional distinctions. But it has to be added that guerrillas do this only
when they are successful in winning popular support. Failure clearly
destroys no distinctions at all. It leaves the guerrillas isolated and
subject to attacks which will be horrifying to non-combatants only if
the attackers are wantonly careless and cruel. Limited success is a
different matter. It can open the way for anything from endemic
banditry to actual civil war, with the local authorities never certain
just who or how many their enemies are: never certain, either, what

actions against the population might be justified. The problems faced by foreign troops fighting local guerrillas are different again: their very presence is generally enough to extend the limits of guerrilla success in such a way that the foreigners must assume that all natives are at least potential enemies. Foreigners fighting local guerrillas are likely to find themselves driven to justify, or rather to attempt to justify, virtually every conceivable action against a hostile population—until they reach that climactic brutality summed up in the orders issued by General Okamura, Japanese commander in the struggle against Communist guerrillas in North China during World War II: "Kill all! Burn all! Destroy all!"

At this point, the questions of morality in war and of the morality of a particular war come together. Any war that requires the methods of General Okamura, or anything approaching them, is itself immoral, however exalted the purposes in the name of which it is being fought. It is simply not the case that every war requires such methods or that violence has some inherent logic which imposes this ultimate brutality on every combatant. The violence of the guerrillas themselves, for example, takes a very different form. But any effort to destroy a guerrilla movement which has won some substantial degree of popular support is almost certain to involve the indiscriminate slaughter of civilians, the shelling and bombing of inhabited villages (it may even require the development of atrocious "anti-personnel" weapons), the burning of homes, the forced transfer of populations, the establishment of civilian internment camps, and so on. It is no use saying that the guerrillas bring all this on themselves, or on their own people, by not wearing uniforms and fighting set battles. Strangely enough, men seem to prefer to wear uniforms and fight set battles when they can. They fight as guerrillas only when they lack the material resources to fight as soldiers. Guerrilla warfare is a means the weak have invented for fighting the strong. It is not for that reason automatically justifiable: the weak have no monopoly on morality. Nevertheless, it must be recognized that guerrilla warfare is effective, in part, precisely because of the moral onus it imposes on the strong. The popularity of the guerrillas (they are not always popular) forces their powerful enemies either to give up the fight or accept responsibility for actions universally condemned by the moral opinion of mankind. I see no reason not to admit that it is almost always better to give up the fight.

Guerrilla warfare is brutal on both sides, though the brutality of the guerrillas is likely to be inhibited by their need to maintain support among the population. The terror campaigns of even moderately successful guerrillas tend to be more discriminating than those of the authorities, partly because the guerrillas have better sources of information, but also because their enemies are forced by their positions to make themselves visible. Under the circumstances, attacks on local magistrates probably constitute legitimate warfare. Such men have consciously joined one side in a civil dispute and presumably know the risks their choice entails. They are, for all practical purposes, combatants. On the other hand, the arbitrary selection of hostages from unfriendly villages, the murder of suspects and "class enemies," the public administration of atrocious punishments—all fairly common guerrilla practices—are illegitimate actions, inadequately justified by some underground version of the theory of military necessity. Brutality of this sort must be balanced against the brutality of the authorities or the foreigners.

Let us assume that in a particular case the balance favors the guerrillas. It still might be said that this provides no basis for a final judgment. For what if the guerrillas advocate the establishment of a tyrannical regime, while the foreign troops are defending democracy? I cannot think of any historical case in which these two conditions are met, but they are possible conditions and need to be discussed. The view is common enough that the side fighting a just war has greater latitude in choosing means than does the side fighting an unjust war. After all, war is not a game; crucial issues are being decided; sticking to the rules may well be less important than winning. But this is a very unstable position, since both sides always claim to be fighting a just war and so might argue that the limits don't apply to them. The real issue, then, is not whether the justice of one's cause legitimatizes this or that act of unlimited violence, but whether one's own conviction as to the justice of one's cause does so. The very least that can be said is that most often it doesn't. The maintenance of some internal limits of war-making is almost certainly more important than the military or political objectives of either side. Once again, however, exceptions are always possible. One would have to be morally obtuse to insist that near-certainty is certainty itself. All that can finally be said is that there is an extraordinarily powerful prima facie case for *jus in bello.*

I do not mean to deny the possibility of justifying some degree of wartime brutality by reference to the purposes of the fighting. War is never an end in itself, and so it either can never be justified or it can be justified only by reference to ends outside itself. The resort to war is at best a desperate wager that things will be better, men happier or more free, when it is over than they would be if it were never fought. There are times, it seems to me, when that wager is morally acceptable. Then we fight, and since we hope to finish fighting as soon as possible, and since we are convinced that our cause is just, we resort to these means that seem to promise victory. Yet ends, we all know, do not justify *any* means, both because ends are contingent and uncertain (the results of the war depend in large part upon the ways in which it is fought), and because there are other ends in the world besides the ones we have most recently chosen. Unlimited violence, whatever its immediate effects, compromises everyone's future: for some it is a final solution, for others a warning of things to come.

Obviously, judgments of relative brutality are not the only basis of our political choices. We also pay attention to the purposes that brutality serves or supposedly serves; we may even choose, not necessarily rightly, greater brutality for the sake of greater purposes. So a man may decide that he wants to fight alongside soldiers who burn peasant villages, because he approves of their long-term goals or fears the consequences of their defeat. I have only tried to suggest that such choices ought to be worrying (that they do not simply trap us in the inexorable logic of war) and that they have their moral limits: there come moments when the sheer criminality of the means adopted by one side or another overwhelms and annuls all righteous intentions. One further point should be made: even short of such moments, our political choices do not free us from the business of judging. We judge our comrades and our enemies, in the name of ourselves, our comrades and our enemies. "I have to take part in the struggle, not to humanize it," Jean Paul Sartre has said. That seems to me precisely wrong. If one must take sides, it is not in order to escape having to impose limits on oneself and one's comrades, but (in part) in order to do so effectively.

The same argument holds, I think, in those interior moments of war, when officers in the field sometimes face the most difficult and agonizing choices. They, above all, have a clear responsibility to uphold the limits. But it may be the case that only some act of brutality against the enemy will save the lives of the soldiers under their command, to whom they have an even clearer responsibility. Prisoners are sometimes killed, for example, because there seems no other way to guarantee their helplessness and protect one's own men. Whatever one thinks of such acts, when they are literally *incidents*, they are at least understandable. And when the exigencies of each incident are taken into account, they are possibly justifiable: here the end may justify the means. But it is something else again when brutality becomes a settled policy. Then it is probably true that officers ought to disobey, or at least to protest, the commands which follow from that policy (and which are unrelated to the exigencies of some particular situation). They ought to do so even if they still approve of the ends for which the war is being fought. Protest and disobedience are now the necessary consequences of their judgments, the only way they have to "humanize" the struggle.

Even if the lives of one's own troops are spared by a policy of unlimited violence, and even if more lives are spared than are lost on the other side, the policy is not justified. Morality in war is not settled by any single measure; it is a matter of long-term agreements and precedents as much or more than of immediate arithmetic. Here the rigorous "law of violence" comes into conflict with what are more loosely called the "laws" of international society. With regard to these laws soldiers must keep two facts in mind: that war is only a temporary rupture in international society and that it is a recurrent rupture. For both these reasons, it ought never to be a total rupture.

It is never the case that wartime actions are limited only by the force available to one side or to the other. Not that such limits are no limits at all; the second is especially effective. Fear of the enemy often has a wonderfully moralizing effect. We must all pray that we never find ourselves at war with an utterly powerless country, deprived of every retaliatory capacity. Still, many wars will be fought between states of radically unequal strength. In such cases, more than in other types of war, it is enormously important that the moral opinion of neutral nations and of all mankind be mobilized to uphold those precarious barriers, distinctions and limits which stand between conventional warfare, ugly as it is, and criminal brutality. Rather than accept the "logic of war" we must judge every military act by another logic.

It is, to be sure, disturbing to see a few men seize upon this other logic and make it the basis for hysterical and self-righteous denunciation. Moral judgment, like moral choice, is highly vulnerable to distortion. Both can become occasions for the shrill expression of personal malaise. The tensions and ambiguities implicit in the very idea of *morality in the midst of war* are all too easy to ignore. And then moral judgments are made in bad faith. But it is, I think, only another kind of bad faith to refuse altogether to total up the gruesome balance, to apply one's moral reason even to the business of war. Let us judge with due hesitation, judge without certainty; and then defend our judgments with all the passion we can command.

Jan Narveson
Pacifism:
A Philosophical Analysis

Several different doctrines have been called "pacifism," and it is impossible to say anything cogent about it without saying which of them one has in mind. I must begin by making it clear, then, that I am limiting the discussion of pacifism to a rather narrow band of doctrines, further distinctions among which will be brought out below. By "pacifism," I do *not* mean the theory that violence is evil. With appropriate restrictions, this is a view that every person with any pretensions to morality doubtless holds: Nobody thinks that we have a right to inflict pain wantonly on other people. The pacifist goes a very long step further. *His* belief is not only that violence is evil but also that it is morally wrong to use force to resist, punish, or prevent violence. This further step makes pacifism a radical moral doctrine. What I shall try to establish below is that it is in fact, more than merely radical—it is actually incoherent because self-contradictory in its fundamental intent. I shall also suggest that several moral attitudes and psychological views which have tended to be associated with pacifism as I have defined it do not have any necessary connection with that doctrine. Most proponents of pacifism, I shall argue, have tended to confuse these different doctrines, and that confusion is probably what accounts for such popularity as pacifism has had.

It is next in order to point out that the pacifistic attitude is a matter of degree, and this in two respects. In the first place, there is the question: How much violence should not be resisted, and what degree of force is one not entitled to use in resisting, punishing, or preventing it? Answers to this question will make a lot of difference. For example, everyone would agree that there are limits to the kind and degree of force with which a particular degree of violence is to

Professor Narveson is a professor of philosophy at the University of Waterloo in Canada. He is the author of several articles in the area of moral and social philosophy and the author of a book, *Morality and Utility*.

His essay "Pacifism: A Philosophical Analysis" appeared in *Ethics*, Vol. 75, pp. 259-271, copyright 1965 by The University of Chicago Press (Chicago: The University of Chicago Press). It is reprinted here with the permission of the author and **The University of Chicago Press.**

be met: we do not have a right to kill someone for rapping us on the ribs, for example, and yet there is no tendency toward pacifism in this. We might go further and maintain, for example, that capital punishment, even for the crime of murder, is unjustified without doing so on pacifist grounds. Again, the pacifist should say just what sort of a reaction constitutes a forcible or violent one. If somebody attacks me with his fists and I pin his arms to his body with wrestling holds which restrict him but cause him no pain, is that all right in the pacifist's book? And again, many non-pacifists could consistently maintain that we should avoid, to the extent that it is possible, inflicting a like pain on those who attempt to inflict pain on us. It is unnecessary to be a pacifist merely in order to deny the moral soundness of the principle, "an eye for an eye and a tooth for a tooth." We need a clarification, then, from the pacifist as to just how far he is and is not willing to go. But this need should already make us pause, for surely the pacifist cannot draw these lines in a merely arbitrary manner. It is his reasons for drawing the ones he does that count, and these are what I propose to discuss below.

The second matter of degree in respect of which the pacifist must specify his doctrine concerns the question: Who ought not to resist violence with force? For example, there are pacifists who would only claim that they themselves ought not to. Others would say that only pacifists ought not to, or that all persons of a certain type, where the type is not specified in terms of belief or non-belief in pacifism, ought not to resist violence with force. And, finally, there are those who hold that everyone ought not to do so. We shall see that considerations about this second variable doom some forms of pacifism to contradiction.

My general program will be to show that (1) only the doctrine that everyone ought not to resist violence with force is of philosophical interest among those doctrines known as "pacifism"; (2) that doctrine, if advanced as a moral doctrine, is logically untenable; and (3) the reasons for the popularity of pacifism rest on failure to see exactly what the doctrine is. The things which pacifism wishes to accomplish, insofar as they are worth accomplishing, can be managed on the basis of quite ordinary and conservative moral principles.

Let us begin by being precise about the kind of moral force the principle of pacifism is intended to have. One good way to do this is to consider what it is intended to deny. What would non-pacifists, which I suppose includes most people, say of a man who followed Christ's suggestion and, when unaccountably slapped, simply turned the other cheek? They might say that such a man is either a fool or a saint. Or they might say, "It's all very well for him to do that, but it's not for me"; or they might simply shrug their shoulders and say,

"Well, it takes all kinds, doesn't it?" But they would *not* say that a man who did that ought to be punished in some way; they would not even say that he had done anything wrong. In fact, as I have mentioned, they would more likely than not find something admirable about it. The point, then, is this: The non-pacifist does *not* say that it is your *duty* to resist violence with force. The non-pacifist is merely saying that there's nothing wrong with doing so, that one has every right to do so if he is so inclined. Whether we wish to add that a person would be foolish or silly to do so is quite another question, one on which the non-pacifist does not *need* to take any particular position.

Consequently, a genuine pacifist cannot merely say that we may, if we wish, prefer not to resist violence with force. Nor can he merely say that there is something admirable or saintly about not doing so, for, as pointed out above, the non-pacifist could perfectly well agree with that. He must say, instead, that, for whatever class of people he thinks it applies to, there is something positively wrong about meeting violence with force. He must say that, insofar as the people to whom his principle applies resort to force, they are committing a breach of moral duty—a very serious thing to say. Just how serious, we shall ere long see.

Next, we must understand what the implications of holding pacifism as a moral principle are, and the first such implication requiring our attention concerns the matter of the size of the class of people to which it is supposed to apply. It will be of interest to discuss two of the four possibilities previously listed, I think. The first is that in which the pacifist says that only pacifists have the duty of pacifism. Let us see what this amounts to.

If we say that the principle of pacifism is the principle that all and only pacifists have a duty of not opposing violence with force, we get into a very odd situation. For suppose we ask ourselves, "Very well, which people are the pacifists then?" The answer will have to be "All those people who believe that pacifists have the duty not to meet violence with force." But surely one could believe that a certain class of people, whom we shall call "pacifists," have the duty not to meet violence with force without believing that one ought not, oneself, to meet violence with force. That is to say, the "principle" that pacifists ought to avoid meeting violence with force, is circular: It presupposes that one already knows who the pacifists are. Yet this is precisely what that statement of the principle is supposed to answer! We are supposed to be able to say that anybody who believes that principle is a pacifist; yet, as we have seen, a person could very well believe that a certain class of people called "pacifists" ought not to meet violence with force without believing that he himself ought not to meet violence with force. Thus everyone could be a "pacifist" in the sense of believing that statement and yet no one believe that he *himself* (or anyone in particular) ought to avoid meeting violence with force. Consequently, pacifism cannot be specified in that way. A pacifist must be a person who believes either that he himself (at least) ought not to meet force with force or that some larger class of persons, perhaps everyone, ought not to meet force with force. He would then be believing something definite, and we are then in a position to ask why.

Incidentally, it is worth mentioning that when people say things such as "Only pacifists have the duty of pacifism," "Only Catholics have the duties of Catholicism," and, in general, "Only *X*-ists have the duties of *X*-ism" they probably are falling into a trap which catches a good many people. It is, namely, the mistake of supposing that what it *is* to have a certain duty is to *believe* that you have a certain duty. The untenability of this is parallel to the untenability of the previously mentioned attempt to say what pacifism is. For, if having a duty is believing that you have a certain duty, the question arises, "*What* does such a person believe?" The answer that must be given if we follow this analysis would then be, "He believes that he believes that he has a certain duty"; and so on, ad infinitum.

On the other hand, one might believe that having a duty does not consist in believing that one has and yet believe that only those people really have the duty who believe that they have it. But in that case, we would, being conscientious, perhaps want to ask the question, "Well, *ought* I to believe that I have that duty, or oughtn't I?" If you say that the answer is "Yes," the reason cannot be that you already do believe it, for you are asking whether you *should*. On the other hand, the answer "No" or "It doesn't make any difference—it's up to you," implies that there is really no reason for doing the thing in question at all. In short, asking whether I ought to believe that I have a duty to do *x*, is equivalent to asking whether I should *do x*. A person might very well believe that he ought to do *x* but be wrong. It might be the case that he really ought *not* to do *x*; in that case the fact that he believes he ought to do *x*, far from being a reason why he ought to do it, is a reason for us to point out his error. It also, of course, presupposes that he has some reason other than his belief for thinking it is his duty to do *x*.

Having cleared this red herring out of the way, we must consider the view of those who believe that they themselves have a duty of pacifism and ask ourselves the question: What general kind of reason must a person have for supposing a certain type of act to be *his* duty, in a moral sense? Now, one answer he might give is that pacifism as such is a duty, that is, that meeting violence with force is, as such, wrong. In that case, however, what he thinks is not merely that *he* has this duty, but that *everyone* has this duty.

Now he might object, "Well, but no; I don't mean that everyone has it. For instance, if a man is defending, not himself, but *other* people, such as his wife and children, then he has a right to meet violence with force." Now this, of course, would be a very important qualification to his principle and one of a kind which we will be discussing in a moment. Meanwhile, however, we may point out that he evidently still thinks that, if it weren't for certain more important duties, everyone would have a duty to avoid meeting violence with force. In other words, he then believes that, other things being equal, one ought not to meet violence with force. He believes, to put it yet another way, that if one does meet violence with force, one must have a special excuse or justification of a moral kind; then he may want to give some account of just which excuses and justifications would do. Nevertheless, he is now holding a general principle.

Suppose, however, he holds that no one *else* has this duty of pacifism, that only he himself ought not to meet force with force, although it is quite all right for others to do so. Now if this is what our man feels, we may continue to call him a "pacifist," in a somewhat attenuated sense, but he is then no longer holding pacifism as a *moral* principle or, indeed, as a principle at all.[1] For now his disinclination for violence is essentially just a matter of taste. I like pistachio ice cream, but I wouldn't dream of saying that other people have a duty to eat it; similarly, this man just doesn't *like* to meet force with force, although he wouldn't dream of insisting that others act as he does. And this is a secondary sense of "pacifism," first, because pacifism has always been advocated on moral grounds and, second, because non-pacifists can easily have this same feeling. A person might very well feel squeamish, for example, about using force, even in self-defense, or he might not be able to bring himself to use it even if he wants to. But none of these has anything to do with asserting pacifism to be a duty. Moreover, a mere attitude could hardly license a man to refuse military service if it were required of him, or to join ban-the-bomb crusades, and so forth. (I fear, however, that such attitudes have sometimes caused people to do those things.)

And, in turn, it is similarly impossible to claim that your support of pacifism is a moral one if your position is that a certain selection of people, but no one else, ought not to meet force with force, even though you are unprepared to offer any reason whatever for this

[1]Compare, for example, K. Baier, *The Moral Point of View* (Cornell, 1958), p. 191.

selection. Suppose, for example, that you hold that only the Arapahoes, or only the Chinese, or only people more than six feet high have this "duty." If such were the case, and no reasons offered at all, we could only conclude that you had a very peculiar attitude toward the Arapahoes, or whatever, but we would hardly want to say that you had a moral principle. Your "principle" amounts to saying that these particular individuals happen to have the duty of pacifism just because they are the individuals they are, and this, as Bentham would say, is the "negation of all principles." Of course, if you meant that somehow the property of being over six feet tall *makes* it your duty not to use violence, then you have a principle, all right, but a very queer one indeed unless you can give some further reasons. Again, it would not be possible to distinguish this from a sheer attitude.

Pacifism, then, must be the principle that the use of force to meet force is wrong *as such*, that is, that nobody may do so unless he has a special justification.

There is another way in which one might advocate a sort of "pacifism," however, which we must also dispose of before getting to the main point. One might argue that pacifism is desirable as a tactic: that, as a matter of fact, some good end, such as the reduction of violence itself, is to be achieved by "turning the other cheek." For example, if it were the case that turning the other cheek caused the offender to break down and repent, then that would be a very good reason for behaving "pacifistically." If unilateral disarmament causes the other side to disarm, then certainly unilateral disarmament would be a desirable policy. But note that its desirability, if this is the argument, is due to the fact that peace is desirable, a moral position which anybody can take, pacifist or no, plus the purely contingent fact that this policy causes the other side to disarm, that is, it brings about peace.

And, of course, that's the catch. If one attempts to support pacifism because of its probable effects, then one's position depends on what the effects are. Determining what they are is a purely empirical matter, and, consequently, one could not possibly be a pacifist as a matter of pure principle if his reasons for supporting pacifism are merely tactical. One must, in this case, submit one's opinions to the governance of fact.

It is not part of my intention to discuss matters of fact, as such, but it is worthwhile to point out that the general history of the human race certainly offers no support for the supposition that turning the other cheek always produces good effects on the aggressor. Some aggressors, such as the Nazis, were apparently just "egged on" by the "pacifist" attitude of their victims. Some of the S.S. men apparently became curious to see just how much torture the victim would put up with before he began to resist. Further-more, there is the possibility that, while pacifism might work against some people (one might cite the British, against whom pacifism in India was apparently rather successful—but the British are compara-tively nice people), it might fail against others (e.g., the Nazis).

A further point about holding pacifism to be desirable as a tactic is that this could not easily support the position that pacifism is a *duty*. The question whether we have no *right* to fight back can hardly be settled by noting that not to fight back might cause the aggressor to stop fighting. To prove that a policy is a desirable one because it works is not to prove that it is *obligatory* to follow it. We surely need considerations a good deal less tenuous than this to prove such a momentous contention as that we have no *right* to resist.

It appears, then, that to hold the pacifist position as a genuine, full-blooded moral principle is to hold that nobody has a right to fight back when attacked, that fighting back is inherently evil, as such. It means that we are all mistaken in supposing that we have a right of self-protection. And, of course, this is an extreme and extraordinary position in any case. It appears to mean, for instance, that we have no right to punish criminals, that all of our machinery of criminal justice is, in fact, unjust. Robbers, murderers, rapists, and miscellaneous delinquents ought, on this theory, to be let loose.

Now, the pacifist's first move, upon hearing this, will be to claim that he has been misrepresented. He might say that it is only one's *self* that one has no right to defend, and that one may legitimately fight in order to defend other people. This qualification cannot be made by those pacifists who qualify as conscientious objectors, however, for the latter are refusing to defend their fellow citizens and not merely themselves. But this is comparatively trivial when we contemplate the next objection to this amended version of the theory. Let us now ask ourselves what it is about attacks on *other* people which could possibly justify *us* in defending them, while we are not justified in defending ourselves? It cannot be the mere fact that they are other people than ourselves, for, of course, everyone is a different person from everyone else, and if such a consideration could ever of itself justify anything at all it could also justify anything whatever. That mere difference of person, as such, is of no moral importance, is a presupposition of anything that can possibly pretend to be a moral theory.

Instead of such idle nonsense, then, the pacifist would have to mention some specific characteristic which every *other* person has which we lack and which justifies us in defending them. But this, alas, is impossible, for, while there may be some interesting difference between *me*, on the one hand, and everyone else, on the other, the pacifist is not merely addressing himself to me. On the contrary, as we have seen, he has to address himself to everyone. He is claiming that each person has no right to defend himself, although he does have a right to defend other people. And, therefore, what is needed is a characteristic which distinguishes *each* person from everyone else, and not just *me* from everyone else—which is plainly self-contradictory.

If the reader does not yet see why the "characteristic" of being identical with oneself cannot be used to support a moral theory, let him reflect that the proposition "Everyone is identical with himself" is a trivial truth—as clear an example of an analytic proposition as there could possibly be. But a statement of moral principle is not a trivial truth; it is a substantive moral assertion. But non-tautologous statements, as everyone knows, cannot logically be derived from tautologies, and, consequently, the fact that everyone is identical with himself cannot possibly be used to prove a moral position.

Again, then, the pacifist must retreat in order to avoid talking idle nonsense. His next move, now, might be to say that we have a right to defend all those who are not able to defend themselves. Big, grown-up men who are able to defend themselves ought not to do so, but they ought to defend mere helpless children who are unable to defend themselves.

This last, very queer theory could give rise to some amusing logical gymnastics. For instance, what about groups of people? If a group of people who cannot defend themselves singly can defend themselves together, then when it has grown to that size ought it to stop defending itself? If so, then every time a person *can* defend someone else, he would form with the person being defended a "defensive unit" which was able to defend itself, and thus would by his very presence debar himself from making the defense. At this rate, no one will ever get defended, it seems: The defenseless people by definition cannot defend themselves, while those who can defend them would enable the group consisting of the defenders and the defended to defend themselves, and hence they would be obliged not to do so.

Such reflections, however, are merely curious shadows of a much more fundamental and serious logical problem. This arises when we begin to ask: But why should even defenseless people be defended? If resisting violence is inherently evil, then how can it suddenly become permissible when we use it on behalf of other people? The fact that they are defenseless cannot possibly account for this, for it follows from the theory in question, that everyone ought to put himself in the position of people who are defenseless by refusing to defend himself. This type of pacifist, in short, is using the very characteristic (namely, being in a state of not defending oneself) which he wishes to encourage in others as a reason for denying it in the case of those who already have it (namely, the defenseless). This is indeed self-contradictory.

To attempt to be consistent, at least, the pacifist is forced to accept the characterization of him at which we tentatively arrived. He must indeed say that no one ought ever to be defended against attack. The right of self-defense can be denied coherently only if the right of defense, in general, is denied. This in itself is an important conclusion.

It must be borne in mind, by the way, that I have not said anything to take exception to the man who simply does not wish to defend himself. So long as he does not attempt to make his pacifism into a principle, one cannot accuse him of any inconsistency, however much one might wish to say that he is foolish or eccentric. It is solely with moral principles that I am concerned here.

We now come to the last and most fundamental problem of all. If we ask ourselves what the point of pacifism is, what gets it going, so to speak, the answer is, of course, obvious enough: opposition to violence. The pacifist is generally thought of as the man who is so much opposed to violence that he will not even use it to defend himself or anyone else. And it is precisely this characterization which I wish to show is far from being plausible, morally inconsistent.

To begin with, we may note something which at first glance may seem merely to be a matter of fact, albeit one which should worry the pacifist, in our latest characterization of him. I refer to the commonplace observation that, generally speaking, we measure a man's degree of opposition to something by the amount of effort he is willing to put forth against it. A man could hardly be said to be dead set against something if he is not willing to lift a finger to keep it from going on. A person who claims to be completely opposed to something yet does nothing to prevent it would ordinarily be said to be a hypocrite.

As facts, however, we cannot make too much of these. The pacifist could claim to be willing to go to any length, short of violence, to prevent violence. He might, for instance, stand out in the cold all day long handing out leaflets (as I have known some to do), and this would surely argue for the sincerity of his beliefs.

But would it really?

Let us ask ourselves, one final time, what we are claiming when we claim that violence is morally wrong and unjust. We are, in the first place, claiming that a person *has no right* to indulge in it, as such (meaning that he has no right to indulge in it, *unless* he has an overriding justification). But what do we mean when we say that he has no right to indulge in it? Violence, of the type we are considering, is a two-termed affair: one does violence *to* somebody, one cannot simply "do violence." It might be oneself, of course, but we are not primarily interested in those cases, for what makes it wrong to commit violence is that it harms the people to whom it is done. To say that it is wrong is to say that those to whom it is done have a right *not* to have it done to them. (This must again be qualified by pointing out that this is so only if they have done nothing to merit having that right abridged.)

Yet what could that right to their own security, which people have, possibly consist in, if not a right at least to defend themselves from whatever violence might be offered them? But lest the reader think that this is a gratuitous assumption, note carefully the reason why having a right involves having a right to be defended from breaches of that right. It is because the prevention of infractions of that right is precisely what one has a right to when one has a right at all. A right just *is* a status justifying preventive action. To say that you have a right to *X* but that no one has any justification whatever for preventing people from depriving you of it, is self-contradictory. If you claim a right to *X*, then to describe some action as an act of depriving you of *X*, is logically to imply that its absence is one of the things that you have a right to.

Thus far it does not follow logically that we have a right to use force in our own or anyone's defense. What does follow logically is that one has a right to whatever may be necessary to prevent infringements of his right. One might at first suppose that the universe *could* be so constructed that it is never necessary to use force to prevent people who are bent on getting something from getting it.

Yet even this is not so, for when we speak of "force" in the sense in which pacifism is concerned with it, we do not mean merely physical "force." To call an action a use of force is not merely to make a reference to the laws of mechanics. On the contrary, it is to describe whatever is being done as being a means to the infliction on somebody of something (ordinarily physical) which he does not want done to him; and the same is true for "force" in the sense in which it applies to war, assault and battery, and the like.

The proper contrary of "force" in this connection is "rational persuasion." Naturally, one way there *might* be of getting somebody not to do something he has no right to do is to convince him he ought not to do it or that it is not in his interest to do it. But it is inconsistent, I suggest, to argue that rational persuasion is the only morally permissible method of preventing violence. A pragmatic reason for this is easy enough to point to: Violent people are too busy being violent to be reasonable. We cannot engage in rational persuasion unless the enemy is willing to sit down and talk; but what if he isn't? One cannot contend that every human being can be persuaded to sit down and talk before he strikes, for this is not something we can determine just by reasoning: it is a question of observation, certainly. But these points are not strictly relevant anyway, for our question is not the empirical question of whether there is some handy way which can always be used to get a person to sit down and discuss moral philosophy when he is about to murder you. Our question is: *If* force is the only way to prevent violence in a given case, is its use justified *in that case?* This is a purely moral question which we can discuss without any special reference to matters of fact. And, moreover, it is precisely this question which we should have to discuss with the would-be violator. The point is that if a person can be rationally persuaded that he ought not to engage in violence, then precisely what he would be rationally persuaded of if we were to succeed would be the proposition that the use of force is justifiable to prevent him from doing so. For note that if we were to argue that only rational persuasion is permissible as a means of preventing him, we would have to face the question: Do we mean *attempted* rational persuasion, or *successful* rational persuasion, that is, rational persuasion which really does succeed in preventing him from acting? Attempted rational persuasion might fail (if only because the opponent is unreasonable), and then what? To argue that we have a right to use rational persuasion which also succeeds (i.e., we have a right to its success as well as to its use) is to imply that we have a right to prevent him from performing the act. But this, in turn, means that, if attempts at rational persuasion fail, we have a right to the use of force. Thus what we have a right to, if we ever have a *right* to anything, is not merely the use of rational persuasion to keep people from depriving you of the thing to which you have the right. We do indeed have a right to that, but we also have a right to anything else that might be necessary (other things being equal) to prevent the deprivation from occurring. And it is a logical truth, not merely a contingent one, that what *might* be necessary is *force*. (If merely saying something could miraculously deprive someone of the ability to carry through a course of action, then those speech-acts would be called a type of force, if a very mysterious one. And we could properly begin to oppose their use for precisely the same reasons as we now oppose violence.)

What this all adds up to, then, is that *if* we have any rights at all, we have a right to use force to prevent the deprivation of the thing to which we are said to have a right. But the pacifist, of *all* people, is the one most concerned to insist that we do have some rights, namely, the right not to have violence done to us. This is logically implied in asserting it to be a duty on everyone's part to avoid violence. And this is why the pacifist's position is self-contradictory. In saying that violence is wrong, one is at the same time saying that people have a right to its prevention, by force if necessary. Whether and to what extent it may be necessary is a question of fact, but, since it is a question of fact only, the *moral* right to use force on some possible occasions is established.

We now have an answer to the question. How much force does a given threat of violence justify for preventive purposes? The answer, in a word, is "Enough." That the answer is this simple may at first sight seem implausible. One might suppose that some elaborate equation between the aggressive and the preventive force is needed: the punishment be proportionate to the crime. But this is a misunderstanding. In the first place, prevention and punishment are not the same, even if punishment is thought to be directed mainly toward prevention. The punishment of a particular crime logically cannot prevent *that* instance of the crime, since it presupposes that it has already been performed; and punishment need not involve the use of any violence at all, although law-enforcement officers in some places have a nasty tendency to assume the contrary. But preventive force is another matter. If a man threatens to kill me, it is desirable, of course, for me to try to prevent this by the use of the least amount of force sufficient to do the job. But I am justified even in killing him *if* necessary. This much, I suppose, is obvious to most people. But suppose his threat is much smaller: suppose that he is merely pestering me, which is a very mild form of aggression indeed. Would I be justified in killing him to prevent this, under any circumstances whatever?

Suppose that I call the police and they take out a warrant against him, and suppose that when the police come, he puts up a struggle. He pulls a knife or a gun, let us say, and the police shoot him in the ensuing battle. Has my right to the prevention of his annoying me extended to killing him? Well, not exactly, since the immediate threat in response to which he is killed is a threat to the lives of the policemen. Yet my annoyer may never have contemplated real violence. It is an unfortunate case of unpremeditated escalation. But this is precisely what makes the contention that one is justified in using enough force to do the job, whatever amount that may be, to prevent action which violates a right less alarming than at first sight it seems. For it is difficult to envisage a reason why extreme force is needed to prevent mild threats from realization except by way of escalation, and escalation automatically justifies increased use of preventive force.

The existence of laws, police, courts, and more or less civilized modes of behavior on the part of most of the populace naturally affects the answer to the question of how much force is necessary. One of the purposes of a legal system of justice is surely to make the use of force by individuals very much less necessary than it would otherwise be. If we try to think back to a "state of nature" situation, we shall have much less difficulty envisaging the need for large amounts of force to prevent small threats of violence. Here Hobbes's contention that in such a state every man has a right to the life of every other becomes understandable. He was, I suggest, relying on the same principle as I have argued for here: that one has a right to use as much force as necessary to defend one's rights, which include the right of safety of person.

I have said that the duty to avoid violence is only a duty, other things being equal. We might arrive at the same conclusion as we have above by asking the question: Which "other things" might count as being *un*equal? The answer to this is that whatever else they may be, the purpose of preventing violence from being done is necessarily one of these justifying conditions. That the use of force is never justified to prevent initial violence being done to one logically implies that there is nothing wrong with initial violence. We cannot characterize it as being wrong if preventive violence is not simultaneously being characterized as justifiable.

We often think of pacifists as being gentle and idealistic souls, which in its way is true enough. What I have been concerned to show is that they are also confused. If they attempt to formulate their position using our standard concepts of rights, their position involves a contradiction: Violence is wrong, *and* it is wrong to resist it. But the right to resist is precisely what having a right of safety of person is, if it is anything at all.

Could the position be reformulated with a less "committal" concept of rights? I do not think so. It has been suggested[2] that the pacifist need not talk in terms of this "kind" of rights. He can affirm, according to this suggestion, simply that neither the aggressors nor the defenders "have" rights to what they do, that to affirm their not having them is simply to be against the use of force, without this entailing the readiness to use force if necessary to protect the said rights. But this will not do, I believe. For I have not maintained that having a right, or believing that one has a right, entails a *readiness* to defend that right. One has a perfect right not to resist violence to oneself if one is so inclined. But our question has been whether self-defense is justifiable, and not whether one's belief that violence is wrong entails a willingness or readiness to use it. My contention has been that such a belief does entail the justifiability of using it. If one came upon a community in which no sort of violence was ever resisted and it was claimed in that community that the non-resistance was a matter of conscience, we should have to

[2] I owe this suggestion to my colleague, Leslie Armour.

conclude, I think, not that this was a community of saints, but rather that this community lacked the concept of justice—or perhaps that their nervous systems were oddly different from ours.

The true test of the pacifist comes, of course, when he is called upon to assist in the protection of the safety of other persons and not just of himself. For while he is, as I have said, surely entitled to be pacific about his own person if he is so inclined, he is not entitled to be so about the safety of others. It is here that the test of principles comes out. People have a tendency to brand conscientious objectors as cowards or traitors, but this is not quite fair. They are acting as if they were cowards or traitors, but claiming to do so on principle. It is not surprising if a community should fail to understand such "principles," for the test of adherence to a principle is willingness to act on it, and the appropriate action, if one believes a certain thing to be grossly wrong, is to take steps to prevent or resist it. Thus people who assess conscientious objection as cowardice or worse are taking an understandable step: from an intuitive feeling that the pacifist does not really believe what he is saying they infer that his actions (or inaction) must be due to cowardice. What I am suggesting is that this is not correct: The actions are due, not to cowardice, but to confusion.

I have not addressed myself specifically to the question whether, for instance, conscription is morally justifiable, given that the war effort on behalf of which it is invoked is genuinely justifiable. Now, war efforts very often aren't justifiable (indeed, since at least one of the parties to each war must be an aggressor, a minimum of 50 per cent of war efforts must be unjustifiable); but if they ever are, is it then justifiable to conscript soldiers? In closing, I would suggest an answer which may seem surprising in view of my arguments a few pages back. My answer is that it is, but that in the case of conscientious objectors, the only justifiable means of getting them to comply is rational persuasion.

The reason is that, in showing that self-defense is morally justifiable, one has not simultaneously shown that the defense of other people is morally *obligatory*. The kinds of arguments needed to show that an act is obligatory are quite different from those which merely show that it is justified. And, since what has been shown is that self-defense is justifiable and not obligatory, the only conclusion that can be immediately inferred from this is that defense of others is also justifiable and not obligatory. Would it be possible to show that the defense of others (at least in some circumstances) is obligatory and not merely justifiable, without at the same time showing that self-defense is obligatory and not merely justifiable?

The only thing I can suggest here is that the answer requires us to speculate about the obligations of living in a community. If a community expects its members to assist in the common defense when necessary, it can make this clear to people and give them their choice either to be prepared to meet this obligation or to live somewhere else. But a community of pacifists would also be quite conceivable, a community in which no citizen could expect the others to defend him as a part of their community responsibilities. One might not care to live in such a community, but then, a pacifist might not care to live in our sort. When the community is a whole nation of present-day size, it is much more difficult to put the issue clearly to each citizen in advance. But the upshot of it is that (1) the issue depends upon what sort of community we conceive ourselves to have; (2) we do not have clearly formed views on this point; (3) there is no basic moral duty to defend others; (4) we therefore have no direct right to force people to become soldiers in time of justified wars; (5) but we do have a right to deny many basic community services to people who will not assist us in time of need by contributing the force of their arms; and so (6) the only thing to do is to try to argue conscientious objectors into assistance, pointing to all of the above factors and leaving them their choice.

Too much can easily be made of the issue of conscription *versus* voluntary service in time of war. (In time of peace, we have another issue altogether; my arguments here apply only when there is clear justification for defensive measures.) It must be remembered that there is a limit to what law can do in "requiring" compliance, and the pacifist is precisely the person who cannot be reached by the ordinary methods of the law, since he has made up his mind not to be moved by force. The philosophical difference lies, not in the question of whether compliance is ultimately voluntary, since with all laws it to some extent must be, but in the moral status which military service is presumed to have. The draft is morally justifiable if the defense of persons is considered a basic obligation of the citizen. In contemporary communities, it seems to me that there is good reason for giving it that status.

Many questions remain to be discussed, but I hope to have exposed the most fundamental issues surrounding this question and to have shown that the pacifist's central position is untenable.

Richard Wasserstrom

On the Morality of War:
A Preliminary Inquiry

Before we examine the moral criteria for assessing war, we must examine the claim that it is not possible to assess war in moral terms. Proponents of this position assert that moral predicates either cannot meaningfully or should not be applied to wars. For want of a better name for this general view, I shall call it moral nihilism in respect to war. If it is correct, there is, of course, no point in going further.

It is apparent that anyone who believes that all moral predicates are meaningless, or that all morality (and not just conventional morality) is a sham and a fraud, will regard the case of the morality of war as an a fortiori case. This is not the position I am interested in considering. Rather the view I call moral nihilism in respect to war is, I think, more interesting in the sense that it is restricted to the case of war. What I have in mind is this: During the controversy over the rightness of the Vietnam War there have been any number of persons, including a large number in the university, who have claimed that in matters of war (but not in other matters) morality has no place. The war in Vietnam may, they readily concede, be stupid, unwise, or against the best interests of the United States, but it is neither immoral nor unjust—not because it is moral or right, but because these descriptions are *in this context* either naive or meaningless or inapplicable.

Nor is this view limited to the Vietnam war. Consider, for instance, the following passage from a speech given only a few years ago by Dean Acheson:

> [T]hose involved in the Cuban crisis of October, 1962, will remember the irrelevance of the supposed moral considerations

This article appeared in the *Stanford Law Review,* Vol. 21, No. 6 (June 1969), pp. 1627-1656. Copyright 1969 by the Board of Trustees of the Leland Stanford Junior University. The portion included here is from pp. 1636-1656 and comprises Parts II, III, and IV of the article.

brought out in the discussions. Judgment centered about the appraisal of dangers and risks, the weighing of the need for decisive and effective action against considerations of prudence; the need to do enough, against the consequences of doing too much. Moral talk did not bear on the problem. Nor did it bear upon the decision of those called upon to advise the President in 1949 whether and with what degree of urgency to press the attempt to produce a thermonuclear weapon. A respected colleague advised me that it would be better that our nation and people should perish rather than be party to a course so evil as producing that weapon. I told him that on the Day of Judgment his view might be confirmed and that he was free to go forth and preach the necessity for salvation. It was not, however, a view which I would entertain as a public servant.[1]

Admittedly, the passage just reproduced is susceptible of different interpretations. Acheson may be putting forward the view that even if moral evaluation is relevant to the "ends" pursued by any country (including our own) it is not relevant to the policies adopted in furtherance of these ends. But at times, at least, he appears to expound a quite different view, namely, that in the realm of foreign affairs moral judgments, as opposed to strategic or prudential ones, are simply misplaced and any attempts at moral assessment misdirected.

Whatever may be the correct exegesis of this text, I want to treat it as illustrative of the position that morality has no place in the assessment of war.[2] There are several things worth considering in respect to such a view. In the first place, the claim that in matters of war morality has no place is ambiguous. To put it somewhat loosely, the claim may be descriptive, or it may be analytic, or it may be prescriptive. Thus, it would be descriptive if it were merely the factual claim that matters relating to war uniformly turn out to be decided on grounds of national interest or expediency rather than by appeal to what is moral.[3] This claim I will not consider further; it is an empirical one better answered by students of American (and foreign) diplomatic relations.

[1]Acheson, "Ethics in International Relations Today," in M. Raskin and B. Fall (eds.), *The Vietnam Reader* (1965), p. 13.

[2]Acheson's view is admittedly somewhat broader than this since it appears to encompass all foreign relations.

[3]Such a view could also hold, although it need not, that it would be desirable for matters relating to war to be determined on moral grounds, even though they are not.

It would be a prescriptive claim were it taken to assert that matters relating to war ought always be decided by appeal to (say) national interest rather than an appeal to the moral point of view. For reasons which have yet to be elucidated, on this view the moral criteria are capable of being employed but it is undesirable to do so. I shall say something more about this view in a moment.[4]

The analytic point is not that morality ought not be used, but rather that it cannot. On this view the statement "The United States is behaving immorally in the way it is waging war in Vietnam" (or, "in waging war in Vietnam") is not wrong but meaningless.

What are we to make of the analytic view? As I have indicated, it could, of course, be advanced simply as an instance of a more sweeping position concerning the general meaninglessness of the moral point of view. What I find particularly interesting, though, is the degree to which this thesis is advanced as a special view about war and not as a part of a more general claim that all morality is meaningless.[5]

I think that there are at least four reasons why this special view may be held. First, the accusation that one's own country is involved in an immoral war is personally very threatening. For one thing, if the accusation is well-founded it may be thought to imply that certain types of socially cooperative behavior are forbidden to the citizen and that other kinds of socially deviant behavior are obligatory upon him. Yet, in a time of war it is following just this sort of dictate that will be treated most harshly by the actor's own government. Hence the morally responsible citizen is put in a most troublesome moral dilemma. If his country is engaged in an immoral war then he may have a duty to oppose and resist; yet opposition and resistance will typically carry extraordinarily severe penalties.

The pressure is, I suspect, simply too great for many of us. We are unwilling to pay the fantastically high personal price that goes with the moral point of view, and we are equally unwilling to plead guilty to this most serious charge of immorality. So we solve the problem by denying the possibility that war can be immoral. The relief is immediate; the moral "heat" is off. If war cannot be immoral, then one's country cannot be engaged in an immoral war, but only a stupid or unwise one. And whatever one's obligations to keep one's country from behaving stupidly or improvidently, they are vastly less stringent and troublesome than obligations imposed by the

[4]See notes 9-11 infra and accompanying text.

[5] Much of this analysis applies with equal force to what I call the prescriptive view, which is discussed more fully at notes 9-11 infra and accompanying text. Although I refer only to the analytic view, I mean to include them both where appropriate.

specter of complicity in an immoral war. We may, however, pay a price for such relief since we obliterate the moral distinctions between the Axis and the Allies in World War II at the same time as the distinctions between the conduct of the United States in 1941-45 and the conduct of the United States in 1967-68 in Vietnam.

Second, I think the view that moral judgments are meaningless sometimes seems plausible because of the differences between personal behavior and the behavior of states. There are not laws governing the behavior of states in the same way in which there are positive laws governing the behavior of citizens. International law is a troublesome notion just because it is both like and unlike our concept of positive law.

Now, how does skepticism about the law-like quality of international law lead to the claim that it is impossible for war to be either moral or immoral? It is far from obvious. Perhaps it is because there is at least one sense of justice that is intimately bound up with the notion of rule-violation; namely, that which relates justice to the following of rules and to the condemnation and punishment of those who break rules. In the absence of positive laws governing the behavior of states, it may be inferred (although I think mistakenly) that it is impossible for states to behave either justly or unjustly.[6] But even if justice can be said to be analyzable solely in terms of following rules, morality certainly cannot. Hence the absence of international laws cannot serve to make the moral appraisal of war impossible.

Third, there is the substantially more plausible view that, in the absence of positive laws *and* in the absence of any machinery by which to punish even the grossest kinds of immorality, an adequate excuse will always exist for behaving immorally. This is one way to take Hobbes' assertion that in the state of nature the natural laws bind in conscience but not in action. Even this view, however, would not render the moral assessment of the behavior of states meaningless; it would only excuse immorality in the absence of effective international law. More importantly, though, it, too, misstates the general understanding of morality in its insistence that morality depends for its *meaning* on the existence of guarantees of moral conformity by others.

[6]It is a mistake just because justice is not analyzable solely in terms of rule-following and rule-violating behavior.

One of the genuine puzzles in this whole area is why there is so much talk about *just* and *unjust* wars. Except in this very limited context of the relationship of justice to rules, it appears that the predicates "just" and "unjust" when applied to wars are synonymous with "moral" and "immoral."

Fourth, and still more plausible, is the view that says there can be no moral assessment of war just because there is, by definition, no morality in war. If war is an activity in which anything goes, moral judgments on war are just not possible.

To this there are two responses. To begin with, it is not, as our definitional discussion indicates, a necessary feature of war that it be an activity in which everything is morally permissible. There is a difference between the view that war is unique because killing and violence are morally permissible in contexts and circumstances where they otherwise would not be and the view that war is unique because everything is morally permissible.

A less absolutist argument for the absurdity of discussing the morality of war might be that at least today the prevailing (although not necessary) conception of war is one that as a practical matter rules out no behavior on moral grounds. After all, if flamethrowers are deemed perfectly permissible, if the bombing of cities is applauded and not condemned, and if thermonuclear weapons are part of the arsenal of each of the major powers, then the remaining moral prohibitions on the conduct of war are sufficiently insignificant to be ignored.

The answer to this kind of an argument requires, I believe, that we distinguish the question of what is moral in war from that of the morality of war or of war generally. I return to this distinction later,[7] but for the present it is sufficient to observe that the argument presented only goes to the question of whether moral judgments can meaningfully be made concerning the *way* in which war is conducted. Paradoxically, the more convincing the argument from war's conduct, the stronger is the moral argument *against* engaging in war at all. For the more it can be shown that engaging in war will inevitably lead to despicable behavior to which no moral predicates are deemed applicable, the more this also constitutes an argument against bringing such a state of affairs into being.[8]

There is still another way to take the claim that in matters of war morality has no place. That is what I have called the prescriptive view: that national interest ought to determine policies in respect to war, not morality. This is surely one way to interpret the remarks of Dean Acheson reproduced earlier. It is also, perhaps, involved in

[7]See notes 12-19 infra and accompanying text.

[8]But suppose someone should argue that the same argument applies to the question of *when* and *under what circumstances* to wage war, and that here, too, the only relevant criteria of assessment are prudential or strategic ones. Again, my answer would be that this also constitutes a perfectly defensible and relevant reason for making a moral judgment about the desirability of war as a social phenomenon.

President Truman's defense of the dropping of the atomic bomb on Hiroshima. What he said was this:

Having found the bomb, we have to use it. We have used it against those who attacked us without warning at Pearl Harbor, against those who have starved and beaten and executed American prisoners of war, against those who have abandoned all pretense of obeying international laws of warfare. We have used it in order to shorten the agony of war, in order to save the lives of thousands and thousands of young Americans.[9]

Although this passage has many interesting features, I am concerned only with President Truman's insistence that the dropping of the bomb was justified because it saved the lives "of thousands and thousands of young Americans."

Conceivably, this is merely an elliptical way of saying that on balance fewer lives were lost through the dropping of the bomb and the accelerated cessation of hostilities than through any alternative course of conduct. Suppose, though, that this were not the argument. Suppose, instead, that the justification were regarded as adequate provided only that it was reasonably clear that fewer *American* lives would be lost than through any alternative course of conduct. Thus, to quantify the example, we can imagine someone maintaining that Hiroshima was justified because 20,000 fewer Americans died in the Pacific theater than would have died if the bomb had not been dropped. And this is justified even though 30,000 more Japanese died than would have been killed had the war been fought to an end with conventional means. Thus, even though 10,000 more people died than would otherwise have been the case, the bombing was justified because of the greater number of American lives saved.

On this interpretation the argument depends upon valuing the lives of Americans higher than the lives of persons from other countries. As such, is there anything to be said for the argument? Its strongest statement, and the only one that I shall consider, might go like this: Truman was the President of the United States and as such had an obligation always to choose that course of conduct that appeared to offer the greatest chance of maximizing the interests of the United States.[10] As President, he was obligated to prefer the lives of

[9]Address to the Nation by President Harry S. Truman, Aug. 9, 1945, quoted in R. Tucker, *The Just War* (1960), pp. 21-22, n. 14.

[10]Other arguments that might be offered—such as that the President was justified because Japan was the aggressor, or that he was justified because this was essentially an attack on combatants—are discussed at notes 12-19 infra and accompanying text.

American soldiers over those from any other country, and he was obligated to prefer them just because they were Americans and he was their President.

Some might prove such a point by drawing an analogy to the situation of a lawyer, a parent, or a corporation executive. A lawyer has a duty to present his client's case in the fashion most calculated to ensure his client's victory; and he has this obligation irrespective of the objective merits of his client's case. Similarly, we are neither surprised nor dismayed when a parent prefers the interests of *his* child over those of other children. A parent *qua* parent is certainly not behaving immorally when he acts so as to secure satisfactions for his child, again irrespective of the objective merits of the child's needs or wants. And, *mutatis mutandis*, a corporate executive has a duty to maximize profits for his company. Thus, as public servants, Dean Acheson and Harry Truman had no moral choice but to pursue those policies that appeared to them to be in the best interest of the United States. And to a lesser degree, all persons *qua* citizens of the United States have a similar, if slightly more attenuated, obligation. Therefore morality has no real place in war.

The analogy, however, must not stop halfway. It is certainly both correct and important to observe that public officials, like parents, lawyers, and corporate executives, do have special moral obligations that are imposed by virtue of the position or role they fill. A lawyer does have a duty to prefer his client's interests in a way that would be improper were the person anyone other than a client. And the same sort of duty, I think, holds for a parent, an executive, a President, and a citizen in their respective roles. The point becomes distorted, however, when it is supposed that such an obligation always, under all circumstances, overrides any and all other obligations that the person might have. The case of the lawyer is instructive. While he has an obligation to attend to his client's interests in very special ways, there are many other things that it is impermissible for the lawyer to do in furtherance of his client's interests—irrespective, this time, of how significantly they might advance that interest.

The case for the President, or for public servants generally, is similar. While the President may indeed have an obligation to prefer and pursue the national interests, this obligation could only be justifiable—could only be a moral obligation—if it were enmeshed in a comparable range of limiting and competing obligations. If we concede that the President has certain obligations to prefer the national interest that no one else has, we must be equally sensitive to the fact that the President also has some of the same obligations to other persons that all other men have—if for no other reason than that all persons have the right to be treated or not treated in certain ways. So, whatever special obligations the President may have cannot by themselves support the view that in war morality ought have no place.

In addition, the idea that one can separate a man's personality from the duties of his office is theoretically questionable and practically unbelievable. Experience teaches that a man cannot personally be guided by moral dictates while abjuring them in public life even if he wants to.

It is also unlikely that a man on becoming President will try to adopt such an approach unless there is something about the office that compels a dual personality. Common sense indicates there is not. If there were, it would mean that the electorate could not purposely choose someone to follow a course not dictated by the "national interest" since, whatever his pre-election promises, the office would reform him.

But the major problem with the national-interest argument is its assumption that the national interest not only is something immutable and knowable but also that it limits national interest to narrowly national concerns. It is parochial to suppose that the American national interest really rules out solicitude for other states in order to encourage international stability.

Finally, national interest as a goal must itself be justified. The United States' position of international importance may have imposed on it a duty of more than national concern. The fact that such a statement has become hackneyed by constant use to justify American interference abroad should not blind us to the fact that it may be viable as an argument for a less aggressive international responsibility.[11]

If we turn now to confront more directly the question of the morality of wars, it is evident that there is a variety of different perspectives from which, or criteria in terms of which, particular wars may be assessed. First, to the extent to which the model of war as a game continues to have a place, wars can be evaluated in terms of the degree to which the laws of war—the rules for initiating and conducting war—are adhered to by the opposing countries. Second, the rightness or wrongness of wars is often thought to depend very much upon the *cause* for which a war is fought. And third, there is the independent justification for a war that is founded upon an appeal of some kind to a principle of self-defense.

[11]It is probably a reaction to the parochial view of national interest that makes plausible movements that seek to develop a single world government and a notion of *world* rather than *national* citizenship.

In discussing the degree to which the laws of war are followed or disregarded there are two points that should be stressed. First, a skepticism as to the meaningfulness of any morality *within* war is extremely common. The gnomic statement is Sherman's: "War is hell." The fuller argument depends upon a rejection of the notion of war as a game. It goes something like this. War is the antithesis of law or rules. It is violence, killing and all of the horror they imply. Even if moral distinctions can be made in respect to such things as the initiation and purposes of a war, it is absurd to suppose that moral distinctions can be drawn once a war has begun. All killing is bad, all destruction equally wanton.[12]

Now, there does seem to me to be a fairly simple argument of sorts that can be made in response. Given the awfulness of war, it nonetheless appears plausible to discriminate among degrees of awfulness. A war in which a large number of innocent persons are killed is, all other things being equal, worse than one in which only a few die. A war in which few combatants are killed is, *ceteris paribus*, less immoral than one in which many are killed. And more to the point, perhaps, any unnecessary harm to others is surely unjustifiable. To some degree, at least, the "laws of war" can be construed as attempts to formalize these general notions and to define instances of unnecessary harm to others.[13]

The second criterion, the notion of the cause that can be invoked to justify a war may involve two quite different inquiries. On the one hand, we may intend the sense in which cause refers to the

[12]This may be what Paul Henri Spaak had in mind when he said: "I must . . . say that the proposal to humanize war has always struck me as hypocrisy. I have difficulty in seeing the difference from a moral and humane point of view between the use of a guided missile of great power which can kill tens and even hundreds of people without regard for age or sex, and which if used repeatedly will kill millions, and the use of an atomic bomb which achieves the same result at the first stroke. Does crime against humanity begin only at the moment when a certain number of innocent people are killed or at the moment when the first one is killed?" Quoted in R. Tucker, supra note 9, pp. 78-79, n. 71.

[13]This is the view put forward by Michael Walzer in his piece "Moral Judgment in Time of War," *Dissent,* May-June 1967, p. 284.

I purposely say "to some degree" because there are powerful objections to taking the "laws of war" too seriously, particularly if they are to be construed as laws or even binding rules. . . . More generally, there are at least four respects in which their character as laws seems suspect: (1) There is no authoritative body to make or declare them. (2) The distinctions made by the rules are specious and unconvincing; for example, the use of irregular-shaped bullets and projectiles filled with glass violates our standards of land warfare—see U.S. Dept. of the Army, *The Law of Land Warfare,* art. 34 (Basic Field Manual 27-10, 1956)—but the use of an atomic bomb does not. (3) The sanctions are typically applied only to the losing side. (4) The countries involved tend to regard their own behavior as lawful because falling under some exception or other.

consequences of waging war, to the forward-looking criteria of assessment. Thus, when a war is justified as a means by which to make the world safe for democracy, or on the grounds that a failure to fight now will lead to a loss of confidence on the part of one's allies, or as necessary to avoid fighting a larger, more destructive war later, when these sorts of appeals are made, the justification is primarily consequential or forward-looking in character. Here the distinction between morality and prudence—never a very easy one to maintain in international relations—is always on the verge of collapse. On the other hand, a war may be evaluated through recourse to what may be termed backward-looking criteria. Just as in the case of punishment or blame where what happened in the past is relevant to the justice of punishing or blaming someone, so in the case of war, what has already happened is, on this view, relevant to the justice or rightness of the war that is subsequently waged. The two backward-looking criteria that are most frequently invoked in respect to war are the question of whether the war was an instance of aggression and the question of whether the war involved a violation of some prior promise, typically expressed in the form of a treaty or concord.

Two sorts of assertions are often made concerning the role of the treaty in justifying resort to war. First, if a country has entered into a treaty not to go to war and if it violates that treaty, it is to be condemned for, in effect, having broken its promise. And second, if a country has entered into a treaty in which it has agreed to go to war under certain circumstances and if those circumstances come to pass, then the country is at least justified in going to war—although it is not in fact obligated to do so.

Once again, even if we pass over the difficult analytic questions that might be asked about whether countries can promise to do anything and, if they can, what the nature and duration of such promises are, it is clear that treaties can be relevant but not decisive factors. This is so just because it is sometimes right to break our promises and sometimes wrong to keep them. The fact that a treaty is violated at best tends to make a war unjust or immoral in some degree, but it does not necessarily render the war unjustified.[14]

The other backward-looking question, that of aggression, is often resolved by concluding that under no circumstances is the initiation of a war of aggression justified. This is a view that Americans and America have often embraced. Such a view was expounded at Nuremberg by Mr. Justice Jackson when he said:

[14] I discuss this distinction between injustice and unjustifiability at notes 23-28 infra and accompanying text.

> *[T]he wrong for which their [the German] fallen leaders are on trial is not that they lost the war, but that they started it. And we must not allow ourselves to be drawn into a trial of the causes of war, for our position is that no grievances or policies will justify resort to aggressive war. . . . Our position is that whatever grievances a nation may have, however objectionable it finds that status quo, aggressive warfare is an illegal means for settling those grievances or for altering those conditions.*[15]

A position such as this is typically thought to imply two things: (1) the initiation of war is never justifiable; (2) the warlike response to aggressive war is justifiable. Both views are troublesome.

To begin with, it is hard to see how the two propositions go together very comfortably. Conceivably, there are powerful arguments against the waging of aggressive war. Almost surely, though, the more persuasive of these will depend, at least in part, on the character of war itself—on such things as the supreme importance of human life, or the inevitable injustices committed in every war. If so, then the justifiability of meeting war with war will to that degree be called into question.

To take the first proposition alone, absent general arguments about the unjustifiability of all war, it is hard to see how aggressive war can be ruled out in a wholly a priori fashion. Even if we assume that no problems are presented in determining what is and is not aggression, it is doubtful that the quality of aggression could always be morally decisive in condemning the war. Would a war undertaken to free innocent persons from concentration camps or from slavery always be unjustifiable just because *it was aggressive*? Surely this is to rest too much upon only one of a number of relevant considerations.[16]

From a backward-looking point of view, the claim that a warring response to aggressive war is always justified is even more perplexing. One way to take this claim is to regard it as plain retributivism. A country is justified in fighting back because the aggressor hit first. Since aggression is wrong, it deserves to be thwarted and punished. The difficulty with this position is, in part, that retributivism generally is more plausible as a statement of necessary rather than of sufficient conditions. Thus, it would be one thing to claim that a war

[15]Quoted in R. Tucker, supra note 9, p. 12.

[16]G.E.M. Anscombe makes the same point in her article "War and Murder," in *Nuclear Weapons—A Catholic Response,* (1961), pp. 45, 47: "The present-day conception of 'aggression,' like so many strongly influential conceptions, is a bad one. Why *must* it be wrong to strike the first blow in a struggle? The only question is, who is in the right."

was *only* justified if undertaken in response to aggression, but it is quite another thing to assert that a war is justified *provided* it is undertaken in response to aggression. For reasons already stated, I think even this would be unsatisfactory, but it would surely come closer to being right than a view that finds aggression to be a sufficient justification for making war. A number of these issues reappear in the related problem of self-defense as a justification.

In order to understand the force of the doctrine of self-defense when invoked in respect to war, and to assess its degree of legitimate applicability, it is necessary that we look briefly at self-defense as it functions as a doctrine of municipal criminal law. The first thing to notice is that the doctrine of self-defense does not depend upon either typically retributive or typically consequential considerations. Instead, it rests upon the prevention by the intended victim of quite immediate future harm to himself. To be sure, the doctrine is backward-looking in its insistence that an "attack" of some sort be already under way. But the fact that it is not retributive can be seen most clearly from the fact that self-defense cannot be invoked in response to an attack that is over. In the same fashion, the doctrine is forward-looking in its insistence upon the prevention of future harm.

Second, it is by no means clear whether the doctrine can be understood better as a justification or as an excuse. It can be understood to rest upon the notion that one is *entitled* to defend oneself from a serious and imminent attack upon life and limb. Concomitantly, the doctrine can be interpreted to depend upon the proposition that it is a natural, almost unavoidable—and hence excusable—reaction to defend oneself when attacked.

In either case what is important is that we keep in mind two of the respects in which the law qualifies resort to the claim of self-defense. On one hand, the doctrine cannot be invoked successfully if the intended victim could have avoided the encounter through a reasonable escape or retreat unless the attack takes place on one's own property. And on the other hand, the doctrine requires that no more force be employed than is reasonably necessary to prevent the infliction of comparable harm.

Now how does all of this apply to self-defense as a justification for engaging in war? In the first place, to the extent to which the basic doctrine serves as an excuse, the applicability to war seems doubtful. While it may make sense to regard self-defense of one's person as a natural, instinctive response to an attack, it is only a very anthropomorphic view of countries that would lead us to elaborate a comparable explanation here.[17]

---

[17]Such a view certainly exists, however; we talk, for instance, about national pride and honor, insults to a country, etc. One real question is

In the second place, it is not even clear that self-defense can function very persuasively as a justification. For it to do so it might be necessary, for example, to be able to make out a case that countries die in the same way in which persons do, or that a country can be harmed in the same way in which a person can be. Of course, persons in the country can be harmed and killed by war, and I shall return to this point in a moment, but we can also imagine an attack in which none of the inhabitants of the country will be killed or even physically harmed unless they fight back. But the country, as a separate political entity, might nonetheless disappear. Would we say that this should be regarded as the equivalent of human death? That it is less harmful? More harmful? These are issues to which those who readily invoke the doctrine of self-defense seldom address themselves.

Even if we were to decide, however, that there is no question but that a country is justified in relying upon a doctrine of self-defense that is essentially similar to that which obtains in the criminal law, it would be essential to observe the constraints that follow. Given even the unprovoked aggressive waging of war by one country against another, the doctrine of self-defense could not be invoked by the country so attacked to justify waging unlimited defensive war or insisting upon unconditional surrender. Each or both of these responses might be justifiable, but not simply because a country was wrongly attacked. It would, instead, have to be made out that something analogous to retreat was neither possible nor appropriate, and, even more, that no more force was used than was reasonably necessary to terminate the attack.

There is, to be sure, an answer to this. The restrictions that the criminal law puts upon self-defense are defensible, it could be maintained, chiefly because we have a municipal police force, municipal laws, and courts. If we use no more than reasonable force to repel attacks, we can at least be confident that the attacker will be apprehended and punished and, further, that we live in a society in which this sort of aggressive behavior is deterred by a variety of means. It is the absence of such a context that renders restrictions on an international doctrine of self-defense inappropriate.

I do not think this answer is convincing. It is relevant to the question of what sorts of constraints will be operative on the behavior of persons and countries, but it is not persuasive as to the invocation of *self*-defense as a justification for war. To use more force than is reasonably necessary to defend oneself is, in short, to

---

whether this way of thinking ought to be exorcised. In any event, however, countries do not respond "instinctively" in the way in which persons sometimes do, and, hence, the excuse rationale is just not appropriate.

do more than defend oneself. If such non-self-defensive behavior is to be justified, it must appeal to some different principle or set of principles.

There are, therefore, clearly cases in which a principle of self-defense does appear to justify engaging in a war: at a minimum, those cases in which one's country is attacked in such a way that the inhabitants are threatened with deadly force and in which no more force than is reasonably necessary is employed to terminate the attack.

One might argue, of course, for some of the reasons discussed above, that this is too restrictive a range for the legitimate application of the principle. More specifically, it might be observed that I have provided an unduly restricted account of the cases in which the use of deadly force is permissible in our legal system; namely, to defend certain classes of third parties from attacks threatening serious bodily harm or death, and to prevent the commission of certain felonies. These, clearly, would also have ostensibly important applications to the justifiable use of deadly force in the international setting. I shall return to this point when I discuss the problem of war and the death of innocent persons in part IV. At present, however, I want to consider an argument for refusing to accord any legitimacy whatsoever to an appeal to self-defense. The argument is a version of what can appropriately be called the pacifist position. The formulation I have in mind is found in the writings of the nineteenth-century pacifist, Adin Ballou, and it merits reproduction at some length. What Ballou says is this:

If it [self-defense] be the true method, it must on the whole work well. It must preserve human life and secure mankind against injury, more certainly and effectually than any other possible method. Has it done this? I do not admit it. How happens it that, according to the lowest probable estimate, some fourteen thousand millions of human beings have been slain by human means, in war and otherwise? Here are enough to people eighteen planets like the earth with its present population. What inconceivable miseries must have been endured by these worlds of people and their friends, in the process of those murderous conflicts which extinguished their earthly existence! . . . If this long-trusted method of self-preservation be indeed the best which nature affords to her children, their lot is most deplorable. To preserve what life has been preserved at such a cost, renders life itself a thing of doubtful value. If only a few thousands, or even a few millions, had perished by the two edged sword; if innocence and justice and right had uniformly triumphed; if aggression, injustice, violence, injury and insult, after a few dreadful experiences, had been overawed; if gradually the world had come into wholesome order—a state of truthfulness, justice and peace; if the sword of self-defense had frightened the sword of aggression into its scabbard, there to consume in its rust; then might we admit that the common method of self-preservation was the true one. But now we have ample demonstration that they who take the sword, perish with the sword. Is it supposable that if no injured person or party, since the days of Abel, had lifted up a deadly weapon, or threatened an injury against an offending party, there would have been a thousandth part of the murders and miseries which have actually taken place on our earth? Take the worst possible view; resolve all the assailed and injured into the most passive non-resistants imaginable, and let the offenders have unlimited scope to commit all the robberies, cruelties and murders they pleased; would as many lives have been sacrificed, or as much real misery have been experienced by the human race, as have actually resulted from the general method of self-preservation, by personal conflict and resistance of injury with injury? He must be a bold man who affirms it.[18]

What is most interesting about Ballou's argument is that it is, in essence, an empirical one. His claim is not the more typical pacifist claim that there is some principle that directly forbids the use of force even in cases of self-defense. His assertion is rather that the consequences of regarding the use of force as appropriate in self-defensive situations have been disastrous—or, more exactly, worse precisely in terms of the preservation of human life than would have been the case if the use of force even in such circumstances were always deemed impermissible.

It is very difficult to know what to make of such an argument. In particular, it is more difficult than it may appear at first to state the argument coherently. What precisely is Ballou's thesis? Perhaps he is saying something like this: The principle that force may justifiably be used in cases of self-defense tends to be misapplied in practice. Persons almost inevitably tend to overestimate the imminence and severity of a threat of violence to themselves. They use force prematurely and in excess under an invocation of the doctrine of self-defense. And if this is true of persons generally, it is probably even truer of countries in their relations with other countries. The answer, therefore, is to induce persons and countries to forgo the resort to force even in cases of self-defense.

This argument is something of a paradox. If everyone were to accept and consistently to act upon the principle that force ought

[18]Ballou, "Christian Non-Resistance," in S. Lynd (ed.), *Nonviolence in America: A Documentary History* (1966), pp. 31, 38-39.

never to be used, even in cases of self-defense, then there would be nothing to worry about. No one would ever use force at all, and we really would not have to worry about misapplications of the principle of self-defense.

But Ballou's appeal is to persons to give up the principle of self-defense even if others have not renounced even the aggressive resort to force. In other words, Ballou's argument is one for unilateral rather than bilateral pacifism, and that is precisely what makes it so hard to accept. As I have said, Ballou's thesis appears to be an empirical one. He appears to concede that if only some persons renounce the doctrine of self-defense they certainly do not thereby guarantee their own safety from attack. Innocent persons in this position may very well be killed by those who use force freely. Ballou seems to be saying that while this is so, the consequences have been still worse where self-defense has not been abandoned. But there is just no reason to suppose that unilateral pacifism if practiced by an unspecified group of persons would have resulted in fewer rather than more deaths.[19]

Perhaps, though, this is not what Ballou really has in mind. Perhaps instead the main thrust of his argument is as follows: People generally agree that force should not be used except in self-defense. But the evidence indicates that this principle is usually misapplied. Hence, a partial pacifism, restricted to the use of force only in cases of self-defense, is illusory and unsound. Even if all countries agreed never to use force except in self-defense, they would still be so prone to construe the behavior of other countries as imminently threatening that wars would be prevalent and the consequences horrendous. This is the reason why even self-defense cannot be permitted as an exception to pacifism. Everyone and every country should, therefore, renounce self-defense as the one remaining exception to pacifism.

Again there is an element of paradox to the argument. Suppose it looks to country Y as though country X is about to attack it. Ballou would say country Y should not, under the principle of self-defense, prepare to fight back. Of course, if all countries do follow the principle of never using force except in self-defense, this makes good sense because country Y can rely on the fact that country X will not attack first. So there is no need to eliminate the defense of self-defense. But what if country X should in fact attack? Here

[19]Still another argument against unilateral pacificism is, of course, that there are evils other than the destruction of lives. Suppose, for example, that unilateral pacifism would result in fewer deaths but in substantially greater human slavery. It is by no means clear that such would be a morally preferable state of affairs.

Ballou's advice is that country Y should still not respond because of the likelihood of misapplying the doctrine of self-defense. Once again the case is simply not convincing. In any particular case it just might be that the doctrine would not be misapplied and that the consequences of not defending oneself would in fact be less desirable than those of resorting to self-defensive force.

In short, the case against a limited doctrine of self-defense cannot, I think, be plausibly made out on grounds such as those urged by Ballou. Although a world without war would doubtless be a better one, it is by no means clear that unilateral abandonment of the doctrine of self-defense would have such beneficial consequences. If there is an argument against war, it must rest on something other than the harms inherent in the doctrine of self-defense.

The strongest argument against war is that which rests upon the connection between the morality of war and the death of innocent persons. The specter of thermonuclear warfare makes examination of this point essential, yet the problem was both a genuine and an urgent one in the pre-atomic days of air warfare, particularly during the Second World War.

The argument based upon the death of innocent persons goes something like this: Even in war innocent persons have a right to life and limb that should be respected. It is no less wrong and no more justifiable to kill innocent persons in war than at any other time. Therefore, if innocent persons are killed in a war, that war is to be condemned.

The argument can quite readily be converted into an attack upon all modern war. Imagine a thoroughly unprovoked attack upon another country—an attack committed, moreover, from the worst of motives and for the most despicable of ends. Assume too, for the moment, that under such circumstances there is nothing immoral about fighting back and even killing those who are attacking. Nonetheless, if in fighting back innocent persons will be killed, the defenders will be acting immorally. However, given any war fought today, innocent persons will inevitably be killed. Therefore, any war fought today will be immoral.

There are a variety of matters that require clarification before the strength of this argument can be adequately assessed. In particular, there are four questions that must be examined: (1) What is meant by "innocence" in this context? (2) Is it plausible to suppose that there are any innocents? (3) Under what circumstances is the death of innocent persons immoral? (4) What is the nature of the connection between the immorality of the killing of innocent persons and the immorality of the war in which this killing occurs?

It is anything but clear what precisely is meant by "innocence" or "the innocent" in an argument such as this. One possibility would be that all noncombatants are innocent. But then, of course, we would have to decide what was meant by "noncombatants." Here we might be tempted to claim that noncombatants are all of those persons who are not in the army—not actually doing the fighting; the combatants are those who are. There are, however, serious problems with this position. For it appears that persons can be noncombatants in this sense and yet indistinguishable in any apparently relevant sense from persons in the army. Thus, civilians may be manufacturing munitions, devising new weapons, writing propaganda, or doing any number of other things that make them indistinguishable from many combatants vis-à-vis their relationship to the war effort.

A second possibility would be to focus upon an individual's causal connection with the attempt to win the war rather than on his status as soldier or civilian. On this view only some noncombatants would be innocent and virtually no combatants would be. If the causal connection is what is relevant, meaningful distinctions might be made among civilians. One might distinguish between those whose activities or vocations help the war effort only indirectly, if at all, and those whose activities are more plausibly described as directly beneficial. Thus the distinctions would be between a typical grocer or a tailor on the one hand, and a worker in an armaments plant on the other. Similarly, children, the aged, and the infirm would normally not be in a position to play a role causally connected in this way with the waging of war.[20]

There are, of course, other kinds of possible causal connections. In particular, someone might urge that attention should also be devoted to the existence of a causal connection between the individual's civic behavior and the war effort. Thus, for example, a person's voting behavior, or the degree of his political opposition to the government, or his financial contributions to the war effort might all be deemed to be equally relevant to his status as an innocent.

Still a fourth possibility, closely related to those already discussed, would be that interpretation of innocence concerned with culpability rather than causality per se. On this view a person would properly be regarded as innocent if he could not fairly be held responsible for the war's initiation or conduct. Clearly, the notion of culpability is linked in important ways with that of causal connection, but they are by no means identical. So it is quite conceivable, for example, that under some principles of culpability

---

[20]For a fuller development of this point see Ford, "The Morality of Obliteration Bombing," *Theological Studies*, Vol. 5 (1944), pp. 261, 280-86.

many combatants might not be culpable and some noncombatants might be extremely culpable, particularly if culpability were to be defined largely in terms of state of mind and enthusiasm for the war. Thus, an aged or infirm person who cannot do very much to help the war effort but is an ardent proponent of its aims and objectives might be more culpable (and less innocent in this sense) than a conscriptee who is firing a machine gun only because the penalty for disobeying the command to do so is death.[21]

But we need not propose an airtight definition of "innocence" in order to answer the question of whether, in any war, there will be a substantial number of innocent persons involved. For irrespective of which sense or senses of innocence are ultimately deemed most instructive or important, it does seem clear that there will be a number of persons in any country (children are probably the clearest example) who will meet any test of innocence that is proposed.

The third question enumerated earlier is: Under what circumstances is the death of innocent persons immoral? One possible view is that which asserts simply that it is unimportant which circumstances bring about the death of innocent persons. As long as we know that innocent persons will be killed as a result of war, we know all we need to know to condemn any such war.

Another, and perhaps more plausible, view is that which regards the death of innocent persons as increasingly unjustifiable if it was negligently, recklessly, knowingly, or intentionally brought about. Thus, if a country engages in acts of war with the intention of bringing about the death of children, perhaps to weaken the will of

---

[21]This discussion hardly exhausts the possible problems involved in making clear the appropriate notion of innocence. I have not, for example, discussed at all the view that culpability is linked with the *cause* for which a war is fought. On this view, innocence might turn much more on the question of which side a person was on than on his connection with or responsibility for waging the war. I do not think this sense of innocence is intended by those who condemn wars that involve the deaths of innocent persons.

Similarly, I have avoided completely a number of difficulties inherent in the problem of culpability for the behavior of one's country. To what degree does the denial of access to adequate information about the war excuse one from culpability in supporting it? Are children who are taught that their country is always right to be regarded as innocents even though they act on this instruction and assiduously do what they can to aid the war effort? To what degree does the existence of severe penalties for political opposition render ostensibly culpable behavior in fact innocent?

All of these questions arise more directly in connection with the issue of individual responsibility for the behavior of one's country and oneself in time of war. This issue is, as I have indicated, beyond the scope of this Article. As is apparent, however, a number of the relevant considerations are presented once the problem of the death of innocent persons is raised.

the enemy, it would be more immoral than if it were to engage in acts of war aimed at killing combatants but which through error also kill children.[22]

A different sort of problem arises if someone asks how we are to differentiate the deaths of children in war from, for example, the deaths of children that accompany the use of highways or airplanes in times of peace. Someone might, that is, argue that we permit children to ride in cars on highways and to fly in airplanes even though we *know* that there will be accidents and that as a result of these accidents innocent children will die. And since we know this to be the case, the situation appears to be indistinguishable from that of engaging in acts of war where it is known that the death of children will be a direct, although not intended, consequence.

I think that there are three sorts of responses that can be made to an objection of this sort. In the first place, in a quite straightforward sense the highway does not, typically, cause the death of the innocent passenger; the careless driver or the defective tire does. But it is the intentional bombing of the heavily populated city that does cause the death of the children who live in the city.

In the second place, it is one thing to act where one knows that certain more or less identifiable persons will be killed (say, bombing a troop camp when one knows that those children who live in the vicinity of the camp will also be killed), and quite another thing to engage in conduct in which all one can say is that it can be predicted with a high degree of confidence that over a given period of time a certain number of persons (including children) will be killed. The difference seems to lie partly in the lack of specificity concerning the identity of the persons and partly in the kind of causal connection involved.

In the third place, there is certainly a difference in the two cases in respect to the possibility of deriving benefits from the conduct. That is to say, when a highway is used, one is participating in a system or set of arrangements in which benefits are derived from that use (even though risks, and hence costs, are also involved). It is not easy to see how a similar sort of analysis can as plausibly be proposed in connection with typical acts of war.

The final and most important issue that is raised by the argument concerning the killing of the innocent in time of war is that of the

---

[22]There is a substantial body of literature on the problem of the intentionality of conduct in time of war. Discussion has focused chiefly on the plausibility of the Catholic doctrine of "double" or "indirect" effect. See, e.g., P. Ramsey, *War and the Christian Conscience* (1961), pp. 46-59; Anscombe (supra note 16), pp. 57-59; Ford (supra note 20), pp. 289, 290-98.

connection between the immorality of the killing of innocent persons and the immorality of the war in which this killing occurs. Writers in the area often fail to discuss the connection.

Miss Anscombe puts the point this way: "[I]t is murderous to attack [the innocent] or make them a target for an attack which [the attacker] judges will help him toward victory. For murder is the deliberate killing of the innocent, whether for its own sake or as a means to some further end."[23] And Father John Ford, in a piece that certainly deserves to be more widely known outside of theological circles, puts the point several different ways: At one place he asserts that noncombatants have a right to live, even in wartime;[24] and at another place he says that "to take the life of an innocent person is always intrinsically wrong";[25] and at still a third place: "[E]very Catholic theologian would condemn as intrinsically immoral the direct killing of innocent noncombatants."[26]

Now, leaving aside the question of whether Miss Anscombe has defined murder correctly and leaving aside the question of whether Father Ford's three assertions are equivalent expressions, the serious question that does remain is what precisely they mean to assert about the intentional killing of innocent persons in time of war.

There are two very different ambiguities in their statements that have to be worked out. In the first place, we have to determine whether the immorality in question is in their view "absolute" or in some sense "prima facie." And in the second place, we should ask whether the immorality in question is in their view to be predicated of the particular act of intentional killing or of the entire war. To elaborate briefly in turn on each of these two ambiguities: Suppose someone were to claim that it is immoral or wrong to lie. He might mean any one of at least three different things: (1) He might mean that it is *absolutely* immoral to lie. That is to say, he might be claiming that there are no circumstances under which one would be justified in telling a lie and that there are no circumstances under which it would, morally speaking, be better to lie than to tell the truth. (2) Or he might mean that it is prima facie immoral to lie. That is to say, he might be claiming that, absent special, overriding circumstances, it is immoral to lie. On this view, even when these special, overriding circumstances do obtain so that an act of lying is justifiable, it still involves some quantum of immorality. (3) The third possibility is that he might mean that, typically, lying is wrong.

23Anscombe (supra note 16), p. 49.

24Ford (supra note 20), p. 269.

25*Ibid.*, p. 272.

26*Ibid.*, p. 273.

As a rule it is immoral to lie, but sometimes it is not. And when it is not, there is nothing whatsoever wrong or immoral about telling a lie.

For the purposes of the present inquiry the differences between (2) and (3) are irrelevant;[27] the differences between a position of absolute immorality and either (2) or (3) are not. The question of the killing of the innocents should similarly fit into the foregoing categories and identical conclusions should obtain, although to some degree the differences among these views and the plausibility of each are affected by the type of activity under consideration. Thus, the absolutist view, (1), may seem very strange and unconvincing when applied to lying or promise-keeping; it may seem less so, though, when applied to murder or torture. Similarly (3) may seem quite sensible when predicated of lying or promise-keeping but patently defective when applied to murder or torture.

In any event the case at hand is that of murder. It is likely that Father Ford and Miss Anscombe mean to assert an absolutist view here—that there are no circumstances under which the intentional killing of innocent persons, even in time of war, can be justified. It is always immoral to do so.[28] At least their arguments are phrased in absolutist terms. If this is the view that they intend to defend, it is, I think, a hard one to accept. This is so just because it ultimately depends upon too complete a rejection of the relevance of consequences to the moral character of action. It also requires too rigid a dichotomy between acts and omissions. It seems to misunderstand the character of our moral life to claim that, no matter what the consequences, the intentional killing of an innocent person could never be justifiable—even, for example, if a failure to do so would bring about the death of many more innocent persons.

This does not, of course, mean that the argument from the death of the innocent is either irrelevant or unconvincing. It can be

---

[27]For discussion of the differences between these two positions in other contexts, see Wasserstrom, "The Obligation to Obey the Law," *U.C.L.A. Law Review*, Vol. 10 (1963), pp. 780, 783-85.

[28]I offer this interpretation because the language typically used seems to support it. For example, Miss Anscombe says: "Without understanding of this principle [of double effect], anything can be—and is wont to be—justified, and the Christian teaching *that in no circumstances may one commit murder, adultery, apostasy (to give a few examples) goes by the board.* These absolute prohibitions of Christianity by no means exhaust its ethic; there is a large area where what is just is determined partly by a prudent weighing up of consequences. But the prohibitions are bedrock, and without them the Christian ethic goes to pieces." Anscombe (supra note 16), pp. 57-58 (emphasis added). And it is also consistent with what I take to be the more general Catholic doctrine on the intentional taking of "innocent" life—the absolute prohibition against abortion on just this ground.

understood to be the very convincing claim that the intentional or knowing killing of an innocent person is always prima facie (in sense (2)) wrong. A serious evil is done every time it occurs. Moreover, the severity of the evil is such that there is a strong presumption against its justifiability. The burden, and it is a heavy one, rests upon anyone who would seek to justify behavior that has as a consequence the death of innocent persons.

The second question concerns what we might call the "range" of the predication of immorality. Even if we were to adopt the absolutist view in respect to the killing of the innocent, it would still remain unclear precisely what it was that was immoral. The narrowest view would be that which holds that the particular action—for instance, the intentional killing of a child—is immoral and unjustified. A broader view would be one that holds that the side that engages in such killing is conducting the war immorally. But this too could mean one of two different things.

A moderate view would be that if one is helpless to prevent the death of the innocent, it is appropriate to weigh such a result against such things as the rightness of the cause for which the war is being fought, the offensive or defensive character of the war, and so on. While there is nothing that can justify or excuse the killing of a particular innocent, this does not necessarily mean that, on balance, the total participation in the war by the side in question is to be deemed absolutely immoral or unjustifiable.

A more extreme view would hold that the occurrence of even a single instance of immorality makes the entire act of fighting the war unjustifiable. Thus, the murder of innocent persons is absolutely immoral in not one but two quite different senses.

My own view is that as a theoretical matter an absolutist position is even less convincing here. Given the number of criteria that are relevant to the moral assessment of any war and given the great number of persons involved in and the extended duration of most wars, it would be false to the complexity of the issues to suppose that so immediately simple a solution were possible.

But having said all of this, *the practical*, as opposed to the theoretical, thrust of the argument is virtually unabated. If wars were conducted, or were likely to be conducted, so as to produce only the occasional intentional killing of the innocent, that would be one thing. We could then say with some confidence that on this ground at least wars can hardly be condemned out of hand. Unfortunately, though, mankind no longer lives in such a world and, as a result, the argument from the death of the innocent has become increasingly more convincing. The intentional, or at least knowing, killing of the innocent on a large scale became a practically necessary feature of war with the advent of air warfare. And the genuinely indiscriminate killing of very great numbers of innocent persons is the dominant legacy of the birth of thermonuclear weapons. At this stage the argument from the death of the innocent moves appreciably closer to becoming a decisive objection to war. For even if we reject, as I have argued we should, both absolutist interpretations of the argument, the core of truth that remains is the insistence that in war, no less than elsewhere, the knowing killing of the innocent is an evil that throws up the heaviest of justificatory burdens. My own view is that in any major war that can or will be fought today, none of those considerations that can sometimes justify engaging in war will in fact come close to meeting this burden. But even if I am wrong, the argument from the death of the innocent does, I believe, make it clear both where the burden is and how unlikely it is today to suppose that it can be honestly discharged.

The International Tribunal at Nuremberg

Judgment and Opinion

The Charter Provisions

---

102   The individual defendants are indicated under Article 6 of the Charter, which is as follows:

Article 6. The Tribunal established by the agreement referred to in Article 1 hereof for the trial and punishment of the major war criminals of the European Axis countries shall have the power to try and punish persons who, acting in the interests of the European Axis countries, whether as individuals or as members of organizations, committed any of the following crimes:

The following acts, or any of them, are crimes coming within the jurisdiction of the Tribunal for which there shall be individual responsibility.

(a) Crimes against peace: Namely, planning, preparation, initiation, or waging of a war of aggression, or a war in violation of international treaties, agreements, or assurances, or participation in a common plan or conspiracy for the accomplishment of any of the foregoing.

(b) War crimes: Namely, violations of the laws or customs of war. Such violations shall include, but not be limited to, murder, ill-treatment or deportation to slave labor or for any other purpose of civilian population of or in occupied territory, murder or ill-treatment of prisoners of war or persons on the seas, killing of hostages, plunder of public or private property, wanton destruction of cities, towns, or villages, or devastation not justified by military necessity.

(c) Crimes against humanity: Namely, murder, extermination, enslavement, deportation, and other inhumane acts committed against any civilian population, before or during the war, or persecutions on political, racial, or religious grounds in execution of or in connection with any crime within the jurisdiction of the Tribunal, whether or not in violation of the domestic law of the country where perpetrated.

The Judgment of the International Tribunal at Nuremberg (Washington, D.C.: United States Government Printing Office, 1947), pp. 3-4, 48-56, 82-84.

Leaders, organizers, instigators, and accomplices participating in the formulation or execution of a common plan or conspiracy to commit any of the foregoing crimes are responsible for all acts performed by any persons in execution of such plan.

These provisions are binding upon the Tribunal as the law to be applied to the case. The Tribunal will later discuss them in more detail; but, before doing so, it is necessary to review the facts. For the purpose of showing the background of the aggressive war and war crimes charged in the indictment, the Tribunal will begin by reviewing some of the events that followed the First World War, and in particular, by tracing the growth of the Nazi Party under Hitler's leadership to a position of supreme power from which it controlled the destiny of the whole German people, and paved the way for the alleged commission of all the crimes charged against the defendants. . . .

The Law of the Charter

The jurisdiction of the Tribunal is defined in the Agreement and Charter, and the crimes coming within the jurisdiction of the Tribunal, for which there shall be individual responsibility, are set out in Article 6. The law of the Charter is decisive, and binding upon the Tribunal.

The making of the Charter was the exercise of the sovereign legislative power by the countries to which the German Reich unconditionally surrendered; and the undoubted right of these countries to legislate for the occupied territories has been recognized by the civilized world. The Charter is not an arbitrary exercise of power on the part of the victorious nations, but in the view of the Tribunal, as will be shown, it is the expression of international law existing at the time of its creation; and to that extent is itself a contribution to international law.

The Signatory Powers created this Tribunal, defined the law it was to administer, and made regulations for the proper conduct of the trial. In doing so, they have done together what any one of them might have done singly; for it is not to be doubted that any nation has the right thus to set up special courts to administer law. With regard to the constitution of the court, all that the defendants are entitled to ask is to receive a fair trial on the facts and law.

The Charter makes the planning or waging of a war of aggression or a war in violation of international treaties a crime; and it is therefore not strictly necessary to consider whether and to what extent aggressive war was a crime before the execution of the London

Agreement. But in view of the great importance of the questions of law involved, the Tribunal has heard full argument from the prosecution and the defense, and will express its view on the matter.

It was urged on behalf of the defendants that a fundamental principle of all law—international and domestic—is that there can be no punishment of crime without a preexisting law. *"Nullum crimen sine lege, nulla poena sine lege."* It was submitted that *ex post facto* punishment is abhorrent to the law of all civilized nations, that no sovereign power had made aggressive war a crime at the time the alleged criminal acts were committed, that no statute had defined aggressive war, that no penalty had been fixed for its commission, and no court had been created to try and punish offenders.

In the first place, it is to be observed that the maxim *nullum crimen sine lege* is not a limitation of sovereignty, but is in general a principle of justice. To assert that it is unjust to punish those who in defiance of treaties and assurances have attacked neighboring states without warning is obviously untrue, for in such circumstances the attacker must know that he is doing wrong, and so far from it being unjust to punish him, it would be unjust if his wrong were allowed to go unpunished. Occupying the positions they did in the government of Germany, the defendants, or at least some of them, must have known of the treaties signed by Germany, outlawing recourse to war for the settlement of international disputes; they must have known that they were acting in defiance of all international law when in complete deliberation they carried out their designs of invasion and aggression. On this view of the case alone, it would appear that the maxim has no application to the present facts.

This view is strongly reinforced by a consideration of the state of international law in 1939, so far as aggressive war is concerned. The General Treaty for the Renunciation of War of August 27, 1928, more generally known as the Pact of Paris or the Kellogg-Briand Pact, was binding on 63 nations, including Germany, Italy, and Japan at the outbreak of war in 1939. In the preamble, the signatories declared that they were—

Deeply sensible of their solemn duty to promote the welfare of mankind; persuaded that the time has come when a frank renunciation of war as an instrument of national policy should be made to the end that the peaceful and friendly relations now existing between their peoples should be perpetuated . . . all changes in their relations with one another should be sought only by pacific means . . . thus uniting civilized nations of the world in a common renunciation of war as an instrument of their national policy . . .

The first two articles are as follows:

Article I. The High Contracting Parties solemnly declare in the names of their respective peoples that they condemn recourse to war for the solution of international controversies and renounce it as an instrument of national policy in their relations to one another.

Article II. The High Contracting Parties agree that the settlement or solution of all disputes or conflicts of whatever nature or of whatever origin they may be, which may arise among them, shall never be sought except by pacific means.

The question is, what was the legal effect of this pact? The nations who signed the pact or adhered to it unconditionally condemned recourse to war for the future as an instrument of policy, and expressly renounced it. After the signing of the pact, any nation resorting to war as an instrument of national policy breaks the pact. In the opinion of the Tribunal, the solemn renunciation of war as an instrument of national policy necessarily involves the proposition that such a war is illegal in international law; and that those who plan and wage such a war, with its inevitable and terrible consequences, are committing a crime in so doing. War for the solution of international controversies undertaken as an instrument of national policy certainly includes a war of aggression, and such a war is therefore outlawed by the pact. As Mr. Henry L. Stimson, then Secretary of State of the United States, said in 1932:

War between nations was renounced by the signatories of the Kellogg-Briand Treaty. This means that it has become throughout practically the entire world . . . an illegal thing. Hereafter, when engaged in armed conflict, either one or both of them must be termed violators of this general treaty law. . . We denounce them as law breakers.

But it is argued that the pact does not expressly enact that such wars are crimes, or set up courts to try those who make such wars. To that extent the same is true with regard to the laws of war contained in the Hague Convention. The Hague Convention of 1907 prohibited resort to certain methods of waging war. These included the inhumane treatment of prisoners, the employment of poisoned weapons, the improper use of flags of truce, and similar matters. Many of these prohibitions had been enforced long before the date of the Convention; but since 1907 they have certainly been crimes, punishable as offenses against the laws of war; yet the Hague Convention nowhere designates such practices as criminal, nor is any sentence prescribed, nor any mention made of a court to try and punish offenders. For many years past, however, military tribunals have tried and punished individuals guilty of violating the rules of land warfare laid down by this Convention. In the opinion of the Tribunal, those who wage aggressive war are doing that which is equally illegal, and of much greater moment than a breach of one of the rules of the Hague Convention. In interpreting the words of the pact, it must be remembered that international law is not the product of an international legislature, and that such international agreements as the Pact of Paris have to deal with general principles of law, and not with administrative matters of procedure. The law of war is to be found not only in treaties, but in the customs and practices of states which gradually obtained universal recognition, and from the general principles of justice applied by jurists and practiced by military courts. This law is not static, but by continual adaptation follows the needs of a changing world. Indeed, in many cases treaties do no more than express and define for more accurate reference the principles of law already existing.

The view which the Tribunal takes of the true interpretation of the pact is supported by the international history which preceded it. In the year 1923 the draft of a Treaty of Mutual Assistance was sponsored by the League of Nations. In Article I the treaty declared "that aggressive war is an international crime," and that the parties would "undertake that no one of them will be guilty of its commission." The draft treaty was submitted to twenty-nine states, about half of whom were in favor of accepting the text. The principal objection appeared to be in the difficulty of defining the acts which would constitute "aggression," rather than any doubt as to the criminality of aggressive war. The preamble to the League of Nations 1924 Protocol for the Pacific Settlement of International Disputes, ("Geneva Protocol"), after "recognising the solidarity of the members of the international community," declared that "a war of aggression constitutes a violation of this solidarity and is an international crime." It went on to declare that the contracting parties were "desirous of facilitating the complete application of the system provided in the Covenant of the League of Nations for the pacific settlement of disputes between the states and of ensuring the repression of international crimes." The Protocol was recommended to the members of the League of Nations by a unanimous resolution in the Assembly of the 48 members of the League. These members included Italy and Japan, but Germany was not then a member of the League.

Although the Protocol was never ratified, it was signed by the leading statesmen of the world, representing the vast majority of the civilized States and peoples, and may be regarded as strong evidence of the intention to brand aggressive war as an international crime.

At the meeting of the Assembly of the League of Nations on the 24th September 1927, all the delegations then present (including the German, the Italian, and the Japanese), unanimously adopted a declaration concerning wars of aggression. The preamble to the declaration stated:

The Assembly: Recognizing the solidarity which unites the community of nations;
Being inspired by a firm desire for the maintenance of general peace;
Being convinced that a war of aggression can never serve as a means of settling international disputes, and is in consequence an international crime. . . .

The unanimous resolution of the 18th February 1928, of 21 American republics at the sixth (Havana) Pan-American Conference, declared that "war of aggression constitutes an international crime against the human species."

All these expressions of opinion, and others that could be cited, so solemnly made, reinforce the construction which the Tribunal placed upon the Pact of Paris, that resort to a war of aggression is not merely illegal, but is criminal. The prohibition of aggressive war demanded by the conscience of the world, finds its expression in the series of Pacts and Treaties to which the Tribunal has just referred.

It is also important to remember that Article 227 of the Treaty of Versailles provided for the constitution of a special tribunal, composed of representatives of five of the Allied and Associated Powers which had been belligerents in the First World War opposed to Germany, to try the former German Emperor "for a supreme offense against international morality and the sanctity of treaties." The purpose of this trial was expressed to be "to vindicate the solemn obligations of international undertakings, and the validity of international morality." In Article 228 of the Treaty the German Government expressly recognized the right of the Allied Powers "to bring before military tribunals persons accused of having committed acts of violation of the laws and customs of war."

It was submitted that international law is concerned with the actions of sovereign States, and provides no punishment for individuals; and further, that where the act in question is an act of State, those who carry it out are not personally responsible, but are protected by the doctrine of the sovereignty of the State. In the opinion of the Tribunal, both these submissions must be rejected. That international law imposes duties and liabilities upon individuals as well as upon states has long been recognized. In the recent case of

Ex parte Quirin (1942 317 U.S. 1), before the Supreme Court of the United States, persons were charged during the war with landing in the United States for purposes of spying and sabotage. The late Chief Justice Stone, speaking for the court, said:

From the very beginning of its history this Court has applied the law of war as including that part of the law of nations which prescribes for the conduct of war, the status, rights, and duties of enemy nations as well as enemy individuals.

He went on to give a list of cases tried by the courts, where individual offenders were charged with offenses against the laws of nations, and particularly the laws of war. Many other authorities could be cited, but enough has been said to show that individuals can be punished for violations of international law. Crimes against international law are committed by men, not by abstract entities, and only by punishing individuals who commit such crimes can the provisions of international law be enforced.

The provisions of Article 228 of the Treaty of Versailles already referred to illustrate and enforce this view of individual responsibility.

The principle of international law, which under certain circumstances, protects the representatives of a State, cannot be applied to acts which are condemned as criminal by international law. The authors of these acts cannot shelter themselves behind their official position in order to be freed from punishment in appropriate proceedings. Article 7 of the Charter expressly declares:

The official position of defendants, whether as heads of State, or responsible officials of government departments, shall not be considered as freeing them from responsibility, or mitigating punishment.

On the other hand the very essence of the Charter is that individuals have international duties which transcend the national obligations of obedience imposed by the individual State. He who violates the laws of war cannot obtain immunity while acting in pursuance of the authority of the State if the State in authorizing action moves outside its competence under international law.

It was also submitted on behalf of most of these defendants that in doing what they did they were acting under the orders of Hitler, and therefore cannot be held responsible for the acts committed by them in carrying out these orders. The Charter specifically provides in Article 8:

The fact that the defendant acted pursuant to order of his Government or of a superior shall not free him from responsibility, but may be considered in mitigation of punishment.

The provisions of this Article are in conformity with the law of all nations. That a soldier was ordered to kill or torture in violation of the international law of war has never been recognized as a defense of such acts of brutality, though, as the Charter here provides, the order may be urged in mitigation of the punishment. The true test, which is found in varying degrees in the criminal law of most nations, is not the existence of the order, but whether moral choice was in fact possible.

The Law as to the Common Plan or Conspiracy

In the previous recital of the facts relating to aggressive war, it is clear that planning and preparation had been carried out in the most systematic way at every stage of the history.

Planning and preparation are essential to the making of war. In the opinion of the Tribunal aggressive war is a crime under international law. The Charter defines this offense as planning, preparation, initiation, or waging of a war of aggression "or participation in a common plan or conspiracy for the accomplishment . . . of the foregoing." The indictment follows this distinction. Count one charges the common plan or conspiracy. Count two charges the planning and waging of war. The same evidence has been introduced to support both counts. We shall therefore discuss both counts together, as they are in substance the same. The defendants have been charged under both counts, and their guilt under each count must be determined.

The "common plan or conspiracy" charged in the indictment covers 25 years, from the formation of the Nazi Party in 1919 to the end of the war in 1945. The party is spoken of as "the instrument of cohesion among the defendants" for carrying out the purposes of the conspiracy—the overthrowing of the Treaty of Versailles, acquiring territory lost by Germany in the last war and "lebensraum" in Europe, by the use, if necessary, of armed force, of aggressive war. The "seizure of power" by the Nazis, the use of terror, the destruction of trade unions, the attack on Christian teaching and on churches, the persecution of the Jews, the regimentation of youth—all these are said to be steps deliberately taken to carry out the common plan. It found expression, so it is alleged, in secret rearmament, the withdrawal by Germany from the Disarmament Conference and the League of Nations, universal

military service, and seizure of the Rhineland. Finally, according to
the indictment, aggressive action was planned and carried out against
Austria and Czechoslovakia in 1936-38, followed by the planning
and waging of war against Poland; and, successively, against ten
other countries.

The prosecution says, in effect, that any significant participation
in the affairs of the Nazi Party or government is evidence of a
participation in a conspiracy that is in itself criminal. Conspiracy is
not defined in the Charter. But in the opinion of the Tribunal the
conspiracy must be clearly outlined in its criminal purpose. It must
not be too far removed from the time of decision and of action. The
planning, to be criminal, must not rest merely on the declarations of
a party program, such as are found in the 25 points of the Nazi
Party, announced in 1920, or the political affirmations expressed in
"Mein Kampf" in later years. The Tribunal must examine whether a
concrete plan to wage war existed, and determine the participants in
that concrete plan.

It is not necessary to decide whether a single master conspiracy
between the defendants has been established by the evidence. The
seizure of power by the Nazi Party, and the subsequent domination
by the Nazi State of all spheres of economic and social life must of
course be remembered when the later plans for waging war are
examined. That plans were made to wage wars, as early as
November 5, 1937, and probably before that, is apparent. And
thereafter, such preparations continued in many directions, and
against the peace of many countries. Indeed the threat of war—and
war itself if necessary—was an integral part of the Nazi policy. But
the evidence establishes with certainty the existence of many
separate plans rather than a single conspiracy embracing them all.
That Germany was rapidly moving to complete dictatorship from
the moment that the Nazis seized power, and progressively in the
direction of war, has been overwhelmingly shown in the ordered
sequence of aggressive acts and wars already set out in this judgment.

In the opinion of the Tribunal, the evidence establishes the
common planning to prepare and wage war by certain of the
defendants. It is immaterial to consider whether a single conspiracy
to the extent and over the time set out in the indictment has been
conclusively proved. Continued planning, with aggressive war as the
objective, has been established beyond doubt. The truth of the
situation was well stated by Paul Schmidt, official interpreter of the
German Foreign Office, as follows:

*The general objectives of the Nazi leadership were apparent from
the start, namely the domination of the European Continent, to be*

achieved first by the incorporation of all German-speaking groups in the Reich, and, secondly, by territorial expansion under the slogan "Lebensraum." The execution of these basic objectives, however, seemed to be characterized by improvisation. Each succeeding step was apparently carried out as each new situation arose, but all consistent with the ultimate objectives mentioned above.

The argument that such common planning cannot exist where there is complete dictatorship is unsound. A plan in the execution of which a number of persons participate is still a plan, even though conceived by only one of them; and those who execute the plan do not avoid responsibility by showing that they acted under the direction of the man who conceived it. Hitler could not make aggressive war by himself. He had to have the cooperation of statesmen, military leaders, diplomats, and businessmen. When they, with knowledge of his aims, gave him their cooperation, they made themselves parties to the plan he had initiated. They are not to be deemed innocent because Hitler made use of them, if they knew what they were doing. That they were assigned to their tasks by a dictator does not absolve them from responsibility for their acts. The relation of leader and follower does not preclude responsibility here any more than it does in the comparable tyranny of organized domestic crime.

Count one, however, charges not only the conspiracy to commit aggressive war, but also to commit war crimes and crimes against humanity. But the Charter does not define as a separate crime any conspiracy except the one to commit acts of aggressive war. Article 6 of the Charter provides:

Leaders, organizers, instigators, and accomplices participating in the formulation or execution of a common plan or conspiracy to commit any of the foregoing crimes are responsible for all acts performed by any persons in execution of such plan.

In the opinion of the Tribunal, these words do not add a new and separate crime to those already listed. The words are designed to establish the responsibility of persons participating in a common plan. The Tribunal will therefore disregard the charges in count one that the defendants conspired to commit war crimes and crimes against humanity, and will consider only the common plan to prepare, initiate and wage aggressive war. . . .

The Law Relating to War Crimes and Crimes against Humanity

Article 6 of the Charter provides:

(b) War crimes: Namely, violations of the laws or customs of war. Such violations shall include, but not be limited to, murder, ill-treatment or deportation to slave labor or for any other purpose of civilian population of or in occupied territory, murder or ill-treatment of prisoners of war or persons on the seas, killing of hostages, plunder of public or private property, wanton destruction of cities, towns, or villages, or devastation not justified by military necessity.

(c) Crimes against humanity: Namely, murder, extermination, enslavement, deportation, and other inhuman acts committed against any civilian population, before or during the war, or persecutions on political, racial, or religious grounds in execution of or in connection with any crime within the jurisdiction of the Tribunal, whether or not in violation of the domestic law of the country where perpetrated.

As heretofore stated, the Charter does not define as a separate crime any conspiracy except the one set out in Article 6 (a), dealing with crimes against peace.

The Tribunal is of course bound by the Charter, in the definition which it gives both of war crimes and crimes against humanity. With respect to war crimes, however, as has already been pointed out, the crimes defined by Article 6, section (b), of the Charter were already recognized as war crimes under international law. They were covered by Articles 46, 50, 52, and 56 of the Hague Convention of 1907, and Articles 2, 3, 4, 46, and 51 of the Geneva Convention of 1929. That violation of these provisions constituted crimes for which the guilty individuals were punishable is too well settled to admit of argument.

But it is argued that the Hague Convention does not apply in this case, because of the "general participation" clause in Article 2 of the Hague Convention of 1907. That clause provided:

The provisions contained in the regulations (rules of land warfare) referred to in Article I as well as in the present convention do not apply except between contracting powers, and then only if all the belligerents are parties to the convention.

Several of the belligerents in the recent war were not parties to this convention.

In the opinion of the Tribunal it is not necessary to decide this question. The rules of land warfare expressed in the convention undoubtedly represented an advance over existing international law at the time of their adoption. But the convention expressly stated that it was an attempt "to revise the general laws and customs of war," which it thus recognized to be then existing, but by 1939 these rules laid down in the convention were recognized by all civilized nations, and were regarded as being declaratory of the laws and customs of war which are referred to in Article 6 (b) of the Charter.

A further submission was made that Germany was no longer bound by the rules of land warfare in many of the territories occupied during the war, because Germany had completely subjugated those countries and incorporated them into the German Reich, a fact which gave Germany authority to deal with the occupied countries as though they were part of Germany. In the view of the Tribunal it is unnecessary in this case to decide whether this doctrine of subjugation, dependent as it is upon military conquest, has any application where the subjugation is the result of the crime of aggressive war. The doctrine was never considered to be applicable so long as there was an army in the field attempting to restore the occupied countries to their true owners, and in this case, therefore, the doctrine could not apply to any territories occupied after the 1st September 1939. As to the war crimes committed in Bohemia and Moravia, it is a sufficient answer that these territories were never added to the Reich, but a mere protectorate was established over them.

With regard to crimes against humanity, there is no doubt whatever that political opponents were murdered in Germany before the war, and that many of them were kept in concentration camps in circumstances of great horror and cruelty. The policy of terror was certainly carried out on a vast scale, and in many cases was organized and systematic. The policy of persecution, repression, and murder of civilians in Germany before the war of 1939, who were likely to be hostile to the Government, was most ruthlessly carried out. The persecution of Jews during the same period is established beyond all doubt. To constitute crimes against humanity, the acts relied on before the outbreak of war must have been in execution of, or in connection with, any crime within the jurisdiction of the Tribunal. The Tribunal is of the opinion that revolting and horrible as many of these crimes were, it has not been satisfactorily proved that they were done in execution of, or in connection with, any such crime. The Tribunal therefore cannot make a general declaration that the acts before 1939 were crimes against humanity within the meaning of the Charter, but from the beginning of the war in 1939 war crimes were committed on a vast scale, which were also crimes against humanity; and insofar as the inhumane acts charged in the indictment, and committed after the beginning of the war, did not constitute war crimes, they were all committed in execution of, or in connection with, the aggressive war, and therefore constituted crimes against humanity.

Guenter Lewy
Superior Orders, Nuclear Warfare, and the Dictates of Conscience

---

The Plea of Superior Orders

Prior to the end of World War II there was no settled rule of
international law on the validity of the defense of *respondent
superior*. The military laws of the major powers varied, Great Britain
and the U.S.A., for example, allowing the plea, and Germany
rejecting it. Article 3 of the Washington Treaty of 1922—binding
only the major powers possessed of capital ships—found submarine
attacks on merchant ships to be a violation of the laws of war
irrespective of whether the attacker was "under orders of a
governmental superior."[1] The London Convention of 1930, on the
other hand, which embodied very similar substantive principles of
maritime warfare, did not include this repudiation of the defense of
superior orders, an omission which informed students of the subject
consider deliberate and indicative of the controversial nature of the
problem.[2]

Early English law had posited the absolutely binding character of
military orders. The military code of 1749 made obedience extend
to *lawful* orders only, but this provision was withdrawn again in the
1914 edition of the *Manual of Military Law*. Article 443 returned to
the doctrine of unconditional obedience and of absolute

Guenter Lewy is a professor of government at the University of Massachusetts. He is the author of two books, *Constitutionalism and Statecraft during
the Golden Age of Spain: A Study of the Political Philosophy of Juan
Mariana, S.J.* (1960) and *The Catholic Church and Nazi Germany* (1964), as
well as a number of articles in political theory.
This essay appeared in *The American Political Science Review,* Vol. 55
(1961), pp. 3-23. Copyright 1961 by The American Political Science Association. The portions included here are from pp. 5-13, 21-23, and are reprinted
with the permission of the author and *The American Political Science Review.*
The footnotes have been renumbered.

[1]Cf. Sheldon Glueck, *War Criminals: Their Prosecution and Punishment*
(New York, 1944), p. 155.

[2]Cf. N.C.H. Dunbar, "Some Aspects of the Problem of Superior Orders in
the Law of War," *Juridical Review,* Vol. 63 (1951), p. 247; J. M. Spaight, *Air
Power and War Rights* (3d ed.; London, 1947), p. 57, hereafter cited as
Spaight, *Air Power* (1947).

non-liability for violations of international law when under superior orders. It reads: "Members of armed forces who commit such violations of the recognized rules of warfare as are ordered by their government or by their commander are not war criminals and cannot therefore be punished by the enemy."[3] The source of the provision was L. Oppenheim's *International Law*, first published in 1906, and a pamphlet authored by Oppenheim and Colonel James E. Edmonds entitled *British Land Warfare: An Exposition of the Laws and Usages of War on Land* and published in 1913.

Article 443 of the British *Manual* remained unchanged from 1914 till 1944. In April of that year the War Office in a complete about-face changed the article on superior orders to read:

> *The fact that a rule of warfare has been violated in pursuance of an order of the belligerent Government or of an individual belligerent commander does not deprive the act in question of its character as a war crime; . . . members of the armed forces are bound to obey lawful orders only and . . . cannot therefore escape liability if, in obedience to a command, they commit acts which both violate unchallenged rules of warfare and outrage the general sentiment of humanity.*[4]

The change had been foreshadowed in the sixth edition of Oppenheim's classic, brought out in 1940 by H. Lauterpacht. But this has not stifled the misgivings of many who see the shift of position as a poorly disguised and self-serving way of preparing the ground for the trials of the German and Japanese war criminals who were sure to invoke the plea of superior orders.

Until 1914 the American military code did not contain any reference to superior orders, though in several judicial decisions that doctrine had been rejected as an unqualified defense.[5] In these judgments soldiers were held civilly as well as criminally liable when the orders they had obeyed were later found to be illegal. The basic principle followed was that obedience was due only to a lawful order, although in practice the test of legality apparently did not involve a possible conflict with the international law of war. An order was seen to be legal as long as it emanated from an officer authorized to give it, did not extend beyond the superior's power or

---

[3]Quoted in Glueck, *op. cit.*, p. 150.

[4]Full text of Art. 443 in United Nations War Crimes Commission, *History of the United Nations War Crimes Commission and the Development of the Laws of War* (London, 1948), p. 282.

[5]For a discussion of these cases see Glueck, *op. cit.*, pp. 144-149.

discretion, and did not involve a manifest violation of the law of the land. Most of the cases on record pertain to rather trivial offenses like being upheld in the refusal to obey an order to assist in the building of a private stable for an officer.[6]

The first explicit linking of the problem of superior orders and the laws and customs of warfare is to be found in the 1914 edition of the *Rules of Land Warfare*. Paragraph 347 of that manual, clearly inspired by the British formulation, laid down that "individuals of the armed forces will not be punished for these offenses [against the law of war] in case they are committed under the orders or sanction of their government or commanders."[7] This provision remained in force until November 1944, one year before the Nuremberg trials. Worried experts had pointed out that the earlier formulation "would give almost the entire band of Axis war criminals a valid defense."[8] It was superseded by the following new Section 345.1:

Individuals and organizations who violate the accepted laws and customs of war may be punished therefore. However, the fact that the acts complained of were done pursuant to order of a superior or government sanction may be taken into consideration in determining culpability. . .[9]

The reference to organizations probably adumbrates the declaration of criminality against certain Nazi organizations like the SS and SD by the Nuremberg International Military Tribunal.

While British and American law, as we have seen, accepted the plea of superior orders until 1944, German law rejected it from the very beginning. The Military Penal Code adopted by the Reichstag in 1872 laid down that in case a penal law was violated through the execution of the order of a superior, "the obeying subordinate shall be punished as accomplice (1) if he went beyond the order given to him, or (2) if he knew that the order of the superior concerned an

[6]See William Winthrop, *Military Law and Precedents* (2d ed.; Washington, D. C., 1920), pp. 296-297, 575, 887.

[7]Quoted in Glueck, *op. cit.*, p. 140.

[8]*Loc. cit.* "In view of Nazi excesses," writes Julius Stone, "a conference of Allied jurists were instructed to review their respective national laws on 'superior orders,' then ranging from the Norwegian which excluded the plea, to the French and British and American which admitted it. The United States Rules of Land Warfare were subsequently amended along with the British and French." *Legal Controls of International Conflict: A Treatise on the Dynamics of Disputes- and War-Law* (New York, 1954), p. 362, n. 75.

[9]U.S. War Department, General Staff, *Rules of Land Warfare*, Field Manual 27-10 (Washington, D. C., 1947), loose leaf insert.

act which aimed at a civil or military crime or offense."[10] In 1921 the German Supreme Court relied on this law in the case of *The Llandovery Castle*, a Canadian hospital ship sunk by a German submarine without prior warning in 1918 and with a loss of 234 persons. Two officers of the submarine were on trial for assisting in the machine-gunning to death of helpless life-boat survivors of the ship. They pleaded superior orders, but the court rejected the plea. While military subordinates, according to the court, ordinarily can count on the legality of orders given by their superior officers, "no such confidence can be held to exist if such an order is universally known to everybody, including the accused, to be without any doubt whatever against the law. . . . They should, therefore, have refused to obey. As they did not do so, they must be punished."[11] Germany continued to reject the plea during the Second World War, notably in the cases of captured allied airmen accused of terror bombing. Summarizing the German attitude, Goebbels wrote in the *Volkischer Beobachter*: "The pilots cannot say that they as soldiers acted upon orders. It is not provided in any military law that a soldier in the case of a despicable crime is exempt from punishment because he blames his superior, especially if the orders of the latter are in evident contradiction to all human morality and every international usage of warfare."[12] Goebbels may not have realized that soon the victorious Allies would quote his words and use them to convict the surviving leaders of the Nazi military machine.

After considerable debate the United Nations War Crimes Commission agreed upon the following rule regarding the problem of superior orders: "The fact that the Defendant acted pursuant to order of his Government or of a superior shall not free him from responsibility but may be considered in mitigation of punishment if the Tribunal determines that justice so requires."[13] All of the trials held pursuant to the Charter and Control Council Law No. 10 essentially conformed to this principle. It is due to the disingenuous use of the plea of superior orders by the Nazi war criminals and the vigorous repudiation of this defense by the various military tribunals that the doctrine of the duty of absolute obedience to superior

[10]Sec. 47, quoted in *Trials of War Criminals*, IV, 471-472.

[11]Quoted in Glueck, *op. cit.*, p. 152. The full opinion can be found in Georg Schwarzenberger, *International Law and Totalitarian Lawlessness* (London, 1943), Appendix 2, pp. 128-147.

[12]"A Word on the Enemy Air Terror," *Volkischer Beobachter*, May 28 and 29, 1944, quoted in *Trials of War Criminals*, XI, 168.

[13]Charter of the International Military Tribunal, Art. 8, quoted in Jackson, *op. cit.*, p. 101. Art. 6 of the Tokyo Charter for the International Military Tribunal for the Far East uses almost identical language.

orders today stands largely discredited. The rulings have also shown, however, that the opposite view, according to which superior orders can never constitute a defense, is equally untenable. Despite the restrictive wording of Article 8 of the London Charter, the Nuremberg courts recognized that in cases of duress and error, for example, the plea of superior orders could afford a defense.[14]

The plea of superior orders was raised by the defense more frequently than any other. It was couched in various forms, of which the appeal to the legal nature of the acts committed as judged according to German law, got the most uncharitable reception. It is of the very essence of the Charter, declared the tribunal judging the so-called major war criminals, "that individuals have international duties which transcend the national obligations of obedience imposed by the individual State. He who violates the laws of war cannot obtain immunity while acting in pursuance of the authority of the State, if the State in authorizing action moves outside its competence under international law."[15] The contention that the defendants had acted pursuant to the direct orders of Hitler, the head of State and supreme military commander, was likewise rejected. "That a soldier was ordered to kill or torture in violation of the international law of war has never been recognized as a defense to such acts of brutality, though, as the Charter here provides, the order may be urged in mitigation of the punishment. The true test, which is found in varying degrees in the criminal law of most nations, is not the existence of the order, but whether moral choice was in fact possible."[16]

The rule here suggested is somewhat ambiguous, for even the soldier faced with death, if he disobeys a criminal order, has a moral choice, *i.e.*, between accepting his own punishment or harming an innocent party.[17] But an examination of the full record of the proceedings leaves no doubt as to what was intended. The real purpose as Telford Taylor explained in the *High Command Case,* was to protect those "whose opportunity for reflection, choice, and the exercise of responsibility is non-existent or limited."[18] In a modern

---

[14]Cf. Dunbar, *op. cit.*, p. 251; Günter Stratenwerth, *Verantwortung und Gehorsam: Zur strafrechtlichen Wertung hoheitlich gebotenen Handelns* (Tübingen, 1958), p. 41.

[15]*I.M.T. Judgment*, p. 53.

[16]*Ibid.*, pp. 53-54.

[17]For a good discussion of this point see Morris Greenspan, *The Modern Law of Land Warfare* (Berkeley and Los Angeles, 1959), pp. 493-95.

[18]*Trials of War Criminals*, XI, 373.

military organization everyone is subject to orders. Yet whereas one can hardly expect a private soldier, drafted into the armed forces and ignorant of the law of war, to screen the orders of superiors for questionable points of legality, the same excuse is not available to those in responsible positions, whose duty it is to ensure the preservation of honorable military traditions. Moreover, most of the defendants, part of the hard core of the Nazi party or SS, could not claim in good faith that they had been unaware of Hitler's criminal plans. As the judgment in *The Einsatzgruppen Case* put it: "The sailor who voluntarily ships on a pirate craft may not be heard to answer that he was ignorant of the probability he would be called upon to help in the robbing and sinking of other vessels."[19] The defendants, far from acting under duress, had shared the ideological goals of the *Fuhrer*. They could and had opposed orders when they did not agree with them, but they were unable to produce any evidence of an attempt to disengage themselves from the catastrophic assignments for which they were being judged at Nuremberg. Quite the contrary, many of the most hideous crimes had been committed on the accused's own initiative.

The tribunals recognized that a defendant might legitimately claim ignorance of the illegality of an order not criminal upon its face. "We are of the view," declared the tribunal in *The Hostage Case*, "that if the illegality of the order was not known to the inferior, and he could not reasonably have been expected to know its illegality, no wrongful intent necessary to the commission of a crime exists and the inferior will be protected."[20] But this was not the situation of most of the accused Nazis. Otto Ohlendorf, for example, commanding officer of one of the notorious *Einsatzgruppen*, admitted that, on the basis of an order, he and his troop had executed more than 90,000 "undesirable elements composed of Russians, Gypsies, and Jews and others."[21] He stated further: "The order, as such, even now I consider to have been wrong, but there is no question for me whether it was moral or immoral, because a leader who has to deal with such serious questions decides from his own responsibility and this is his responsibility and I cannot examine and [can] not judge. I am not entitled to do so."[22] The court concluded that in view of this acknowledged unwillingness to exercise moral judgment the plea of superior orders was unavailable.

[19]*Ibid.*, IV, 473.
[20]*Ibid.*, XI, 1236.
[21]*Ibid.*, IV, 134.
[22]*Ibid.*, IV, 303.

"The obedience of a soldier is not the obedience of an automaton. A soldier is a reasoning agent. He does not respond, and is not expected to respond, like a piece of machinery.... To plead superior orders one must show an excusable ignorance of their illegality."[23] This might be the case, for example, when an officer executes an order in the belief that it constitutes a justifiable reprisal against unlawful methods of warfare employed by the enemy.[24]

The legal principles established by the war crimes trials have come in for a good deal of criticism, and this has included their basic thesis that international law imposes duties and obligations upon individuals and that these therefore can be punished for war crimes committed under orders of a sovereign state or their military superiors. The law of warfare, like all international law, is held to be addressed to states and not individuals. So one critic writes:

International law is not in position to protect individuals, wherever they may be, against a domestic law which is illegal from the point of view of international law. According to general legal principles, it therefore cannot expect the individuals to expose themselves to such a risk. For the individual, always and everywhere, national law precedes international law. He has to obey the national law even where it compels him to violate international law.[25]

According to this view, no soldier has an unqualified duty to disobey as long as states exist with a sovereignty of their own and the community of nations is unable to shield a citizen who wants to obey international law rather than the law or orders of his own government.

Given this strong current of criticism—which is not limited to German scholars[26]—the question whether the law of the war crimes

---

[23]*Ibid.*, IV, 470, 473.

[24]Cf. United Nations War Crimes Commission, *Law Reports of Trials of War Criminals* (London, 1947), XI, 25-27.

[25]August von Knieriem, *The Nuremberg Trials*, trans. Elizabeth D. Schmitt (Chicago, 1959), p. 47. The same point is stressed by Hellmuth von Weber, "Die strafrechtliche Verantwortlichkeit für Handeln auf Befehl," *Monatsschrift für Deutsches Recht*, Vol. 2 (1948), pp. 34-42.

[26]Percy E. Corbett, for example, in his *Law and Society in the Relations of States* (New York, 1951), p. 232, argues that the Nuremberg tribunal has ignored "the long and undecided doctrinal debate on the question whether, and how far, the individual is subject to rights and duties under the law of nations. It was also ignoring the negative trend of practice, in which recognition of the international personality of the individual hitherto has certainly been exceptional." See also Hans Kelsen's article "Will the Judgment of the Nuremberg Trial Constitute a Precedent in International Law?" *International Law Quarterly*, Vol. 1 (1947), pp. 153-171.

trials is international law would seem to be still open. The action of the General Assembly of the United Nations on December II, 1946, affirming the principles of international law recognized by the Charter of the Nuremberg Tribunal, certainly does not establish the identity of these principles with international law.[27] The International Law Commission, cognizant of this fact, in its 1950 report merely *formulated* the principles of international law recognized in the Charter and judgment of the Nuremberg Tribunal. It did not evaluate them, realizing that their legal validity had yet to be proven by general acceptance and consent evidenced by conduct.

The need for common agreement on the status of the plea of superior orders is clear: "The cause of humanity and of the development of international law demands that license to commit atrocities shall not indirectly be conferred upon members of the armed forces by permitting the latter to take shelter under the canopy of superior orders."[28] While army regulations are not competent sources of international law, the fact that practically all military codes today follow the Nuremberg doctrine on this matter is to be welcomed as a step in this direction and is of evidential value in determining the existence of usage and practice, an important stage in the crystallization of the customary law of war. The rulings of the Nuremberg trials on the plea of superior orders, in view of the hurried changes introduced in the military codes of the United Nations in 1944, were open to the objection of retroactivity. Given the consensus existing today, it will be difficult to make this same charge in the future.

The most recent edition of the American *Law of Land Warfare* reads as follows:

The fact that the law of war has been violated pursuant to an order of a superior authority, whether military or civil, does not deprive the act in question of its character as a war crime, nor does it constitute a defense in the trial of an accused individual, unless he did not know and could not reasonably have been expected to know that the act ordered was unlawful. In all cases where the order is held not to constitute a defense to an allegation of war crime, the fact that the individual was acting pursuant to orders may be considered in mitigation of punishment.[29]

[27]Cf. Hans-Heinrich Jescheck, "Die Entwicklung des Völkerstrafrechts nach Nürnberg," *Schweizerische Zeitschrift für Strafrecht*, Vol. 72 (1957), pp. 217-248.

[28]Dunbar, *op cit.*, p. 261.

[29]*U. S. Law of Land Warfare* (1956). Art. 509(a), p. 182. Art. 330b (1) of the *Law of Naval Warfare* (1955) uses practically identical language. Cf. Robert W. Tucker, *The Law of War and Neutrality at Sea* (Washington, D. C., 1957), pp. 374-375.

The 1958 edition of the British *Laws of War on Land* is even more far-reaching and entirely rules out acceptance of the plea of superior orders as a defense. Art. 627 provides that "obedience to the order of a government or of a superior, whether military or civil, or to a national law or regulation, affords no defense to a charge of committing a war crime but may be considered in mitigation of punishment."[30] An attached note points out that no mitigating factor will be recognized in the case of military commanders at the highest level of the military hierarchy. "Far from being irresistibly compelled to obey unlawful orders they are in a position, by a refusal to obey them, to arrest or prevent their operation."[31] Following Bacon's maxim that "urgent necessity no matter how grave is no excuse for the killing of another," the *Manual* provides that even peril of death does not remove criminal responsibility for the taking of innocent life.[32]

The relevant provisions of the new military code of the German Federal Republic are based upon Article 25 of the Basic Law (*Grundgesetz*), according to which "the general rules of international law shall form part of federal law. They shall take precedence over the laws and create rights and duties directly for the inhabitants of the federal territory."[33] Military superiors must make sure that their orders conform to international law,[34] and the subordinate is not guilty of insubordination if an order violates human dignity. "An order may not be executed if obedience to it would constitute a crime or transgression."[35] A subordinate who fails to obey an order because of the mistaken belief that its execution would bring about a crime or transgression is not liable to punishment, if he cannot be blamed for the error.[36] The military code of the new West German

---

[30]*British Law of War* (1958), Art. 627, p. 176.

[31]*Ibid.*, Art. 627, n. 2(f), p. 177.

[32]*Ibid.*, Art. 629, p. 177. The English law on the question of duress is more stringent than the Nuremberg trials. The judgment in *The Einsatzgruppen Case*, handed down by a panel of American judges, has asserted that "there is no law which requires that an innocent man must forfeit his life or suffer serious harm in order to avoid committing a crime." *Trials of War Criminals*, IV, 480.

[33]Quoted in Herbert W. Briggs, *The Law of Nations* (2d ed.; New York, 1952), p. 58.

[34]*Soldatengesetz und Verordnungen über die Regelung des militärischen Vorgesetztenverhältnisses* (erläutert von Werner Scherer) (Berlin, 1956), Art. 10(4), p. 4.

[35]*Ibid.*, Art. 11, pp. 4-5.

[36]*Wehrstrafgesetz* (mit Erläuterungen von Gotthard Frhr. von Richthofen), (Cologne-Berlin, 1957), Art. 22, p. 44.

army, one can readily see, leans over backward in order to accom-
modate the individual soldier and to prevent a return to the Nazi
dogma of unquestioning obedience to orders.

The military law of the Soviet Union stresses the duty of instant
obedience to orders but grants servicemen "the right to make
complaints about illegal actions and orders of commanders."[37] A
soldier carrying out the unlawful order of a superior "incurs no
responsibility for the crime, which is that of the officer, except
where the soldier fulfills an order which is clearly criminal, in which
case the soldier is responsible with the officer who issued the
order."[38] After surveying the relevant provisions of many other
national military codes one student of the subject comes to the
conclusion that the principle of unconditional obedience and of
complete freedom from responsibility for superior orders has all but
disappeared today.[39]

International lawyers speak of a custom "when a clear and
continuous habit of doing certain actions has grown up under the
aegis of the conviction that these actions are, according to
International Law, obligatory or right."[40] Since the teachings of the
most highly qualified jurists of the various nations can be regarded as
a subsidiary source of international law,[41] we may turn to them in
order to ascertain the existence of such a conviction. Such an
examination reveals that practically all writers do indeed approve of
the recent formulations which deny that the plea of superior orders
constitutes an absolute defense to a clearly criminal act. Even
authors critical of the way the Nuremberg Courts handled this issue
and skeptical about the principle of individual responsibility agree
that in cases of certain atrocious orders obviously incompatible with
the laws of war the duty of obedience ceases and the subordinate
will commit a crime if he carries out the order.[42] The same view is

[37]Disciplinary Code of the Armed Forces of the USSR (1946), Art. 96,
quoted in Harold J. Berman and Miroslav Kerner, eds. and trans., *Documents
on Soviet Military Law and Administration* (Cambridge, Mass., 1955), p. 70.

[38]V. M. Chkhikvadze, *Sovetskoe Voenno-Ugolovmoe Prava* [Soviet Military
Criminal Law] (Moscow, 1948), pp. 198-199, quoted in Greenspan, *op. cit.*,
p. 491.

[39]Stratenwerth, *op. cit.*, pp. 28-40.

[40]L. Oppenheim, *International Law: A Treatise*, vol. I (8th ed. by
H. Lauterpacht; London, 1955), p. 26, hereafter cited as Oppenheim-
Lauterpacht, I (8th ed., 1955).

[41]The statute of the International Court of Justice speaks of the writings of
eminent publicists in this sense. Cf. *ibid.*, 33.

[42]So von Knieriem, for example: "If in a territory behind the front line, a
local commander orders a Massacre of the Innocents, or if he orders all Jewish
civilians of the district of occupation to be shot for the exclusive reason that

held by Lauterpacht, the most recent editor of Oppenheim, on whose teaching, as we have seen, the contemporary British *Manual* is based.[43] And Dunbar maintains flatly that this rule today "may properly be regarded as forming part of international law."[44]

All authorities stress that the plea of superior orders can be rejected only when the illegality of the act is manifest or if the subordinate could and should reasonably have known that the act ordered was unlawful. This means that the disputed character of some of the laws of war has a direct bearing on the question of superior orders. "If it is true," writes Lauterpacht, that "the obviousness and the indisputability of the crime tend to eliminate one of the possible justifications of the plea of superior orders, then the controversial character of a particular rule of war adds weight to any appeal to superior orders."[45] Does the legality of nuclear weapons, then, fall into this category of controversial precepts of the international law of war?

The Legality of Nuclear Weapons

The question of the legality of nuclear weapons has received surprisingly scant attention from international lawyers. This may be due to a feeling of futility on the part of men who know that the employment of new and decisive weapons or methods of warfare has never yet yielded to considerations of humanity and that the decision whether to use or not to use nuclear weapons most probably will be made on military or political (including moral), but not on legal grounds. There is also the disappointing status of fifteen years of negotiations designed to bring about an end to the nuclear arms race, an attempt which, as Lauterpacht points out, "is not likely to receive a notable accession of strength from controversial assertions as to the present illegality of the use of the atomic weapon either in general or against the civilian population."[46]

---

they are Jews, nobody will believe that such acts could be justified by the laws of war, even though the harshest necessities of war be taken into account. If a subordinate ever receives such an order, he knows that it aims at a crime and nothing but a crime and all conditions of the duty of obedience are removed" (*op. cit.*, p. 244).

[43]Cf. Oppenheim-Lauterpacht, II (7th ed., 1952), 568-572.

[44]Dunbar, *op cit.*, p. 252.

[45]H. Lauterpacht, "The Law of Nations and the Punishment of War Crimes," *British Year Book of International Law*, XXI (1944), 58-95.

[46]"The Problem of the Revision of the Law of War," *Ibid.*, XXIX (1952), 370.

Since nuclear bombs had not as yet been invented when most of the existing conventions regulating the methods of warfare were drawn up, no explicit conventional law presently exists regarding the legality of these weapons. The American *Law of Land Warfare* concludes, therefore, that nuclear weapons are legal or at least not illegal. "The use of explosive 'atomic weapons,' whether by air, sea or land forces, cannot as such be regarded as violative of international law in the absence of any customary rule of international law or international convention restricting their employment."[47] Yet it is doubtful that the absence of an express international agreement or customary rule is as decisive as this formulation would make it appear. This is recognized by the British *Manual* which declares that, lacking a rule of international law dealing specifically with nuclear weapons, "their use . . . is governed by the general principles laid down in this chapter [on the means of carrying on war]."[48] These include the principle that the means employed in weakening the enemy's power of resistance are not unlimited and that "there are compelling dictates of humanity, morality, civilization and chivalry, which must not be disregarded."[49] For a more detailed discussion the reader of the *Manual* is referred to the 7th edition of Oppenheim's treatise edited by Lauterpacht. The latter, in turn, suggests that the question be judged by reference "(a) to existing international instruments relating to the limits of the use of violence in war; (b) to the distinction, which many believe is fundamental, between combatants and non-combatants; and (c) to the principles of humanity, which, to some degree, must be regarded as forming part of the law of war."[50] We will follow Lauterpacht's suggestion and build our discussion around these three criteria.

International agreements limiting the use of violence   Article 23 (e) of the Hague Convention No. IV regulating land warfare (Oct. 18, 1907) prohibits resort to "arms, projectiles, or material calculated to cause unnecessary suffering."[51] All the major powers, including the United States, are a party to this convention. Given the horrible character of nuclear heat and radiation injuries, it may be thought that nuclear weapons violate the rule against the infliction of "unnecessary suffering." In practice, however, the line between

---

[47]*U.S. Law of Land Warfare* (1956), Art. 35, p. 18.

[48]*British Law of War* (1958), Art. 113, p. 42.

[49]*Ibid.*, Art. 107, p. 40.

[50]Oppenheim-Lauterpacht, II (7th ed., 1952), 347-348.

[51]U. S. Department of the Air Force, *Treaties Governing Land Warfare* (Washington, D. C., 1958), p. 12, hereafter cited as *U. S. Treaties on Land Warfare* (1958).

necessary and unnecessary suffering has been drawn in a way hardly suggested by the humanitarian spirit of the Hague Convention. The criterion has normally been whether a weapon inflicts suffering disproportionate to the military advantage to be gained by its use,[52] and this has meant that no militarily decisive weapon has ever been regarded as causing superfluous injury, no matter how painful the suffering resulting from its use. "The legality of hand grenades, flamethrowers, napalm and incendiary bombs in contemporary warfare," notes Schwarzenberger, "is a vivid reminder that suffering caused by weapons with sufficiently large destructive potentialities is not 'unnecessary' in the meaning of this rule."[53] Since nuclear weapons are notoriously potent and destructive, their use would seem unaffected by the prohibition of "unnecessary suffering."

That the law is interpreted in this way is brought out by the American *Law of Land Warfare* which accepts the illegality of "lances with barbed heads, irregular-shaped bullets, and projectiles filled with glass,"[54] but sees nothing wrong with atomic bombs. Indeed, carrying the argument several steps further, it has been suggested that atomic warfare may be more humane than a prolonged conflict fought with inefficient weapons, for it will shorten the war and therefore bring about a return to peace with the least amount of general suffering.[55] This doctrine, originally developed by German military leaders like Moltke and von Hindenburg, is one which Western writers rejected until the use of the atomic bomb against Japan in World War II gave it some respectability. It is clear that, quite apart from the possibility that an all-out nuclear war may not leave any humanity to enjoy the restoration of peace,[56] the acceptance of this line of reasoning

---

[52]Cf. Richard R. Baxter, "The Role of Law in Modern War," *Proceedings of the American Society of International Law*, Vol. 47 (1953), p. 91.

[53]Georg Schwarzenberger, *The Legality of Nuclear Weapons* (London, 1958), p. 44, hereafter cited as Schwarzenberger, *Legality*. My discussion of the legal aspects of nuclear warfare leans extensively upon Schwarzenberger's succinct analysis.

[54]*U. S. Law of Land Warfare* (1956), Art 34, p. 18.

[55]Cf. Phillips, *op. cit.,* note 3 above, p. 409.

[56]Edward Teller wrote in 1947 that an atomic war fought with greatly perfected weapons might "endanger the survival of man," "How Dangerous are Atomic Weapons?", *Bulletin of the Atomic Scientists*, Vol 3 (1947), p. 36. This was written before the coming of the hydrogen bomb. The Nobel Prize-winning nuclear physicist Otto Hahn has stated since that 10 powerful H-bombs, surrounded with a heavy coat of cobalt, could jeopardize the continued existence of the human race, no matter where dropped. "Cobalt 60: Gefahr oder Segen für die Menscheit?", *Frankfurter Allgemeine Zeitung,* February 19, 1955, and this estimate has been accepted by other scientists. For the view that human life on earth can not *as yet* be terminated see Ralph E. Lapp, *The New Force: The Story of Atoms and People* (New York, 1953), p. 97.

would mean the formal end of the entire international law of war.

The argument that nuclear weapons violate the prohibition of the use of poison seems considerably stronger. Article 23 (a) of Hague Convention No. IV forbids the employment of poison or poisoned weapons and this rule today is regarded as so basic to the practice of civilized nations as to be part of international customary law. This means that the resort to poison would not be legal even in a war in which not all of the belligerents were parties to the Hague Convention, thus overcoming the *si omnes* or "all-participation clause" of the agreement. Poison, in contemporary usage, means any substance which "when introduced into, or absorbed by, a living organism destroys life or injures health."[57] Since all nuclear devices, including the so-called "clean bomb," result in some radioactive fall-out which when introduced into the human body in sufficiently large doses, is harmful if not fatal, Schwarzenberger concludes that "a *prima facie* case appears to exist for regarding the use of nuclear weapons as incompatible with the prohibition of the use of poison."[58] There is also the fact that the explosion of bombs yielding large amounts of fission energy causes radioactive contamination over very wide areas and thus would poison the water supply as well as crops. Such measures are expressly forbidden by the military codes of all nations.[59]

It can also be argued that nuclear weapons are unlawful because they are an analogue of gas and bacteriological warfare and thus in violation of still another species of the genus "poison." That high fission content bombs are, in effect, weapons of radiological warfare is undisputed.[60] But even "cleaner" bombs release atomic clouds and gas bubbles which would seem to bring them within the prohibitions of the Geneva Gas Protocol of 1925, which forbids "the use in war of asphyxiating, poisonous or other gases and of all analogous liquids, materials or devices." This agreement binds over forty states, including Great Britain and the Soviet Union. The U.S.A., after signing the Protocol, did not ratify it, and, according to the *Law of Land Warfare*, the United States expressly reserves the

---

[57]*Shorter Oxford Dictionary*, quoted in Schwarzenberger, *Legality*, p. 27.

[58]*Ibid.*, p. 28. See also the detailed analysis in Negendra Singh, *Nuclear Weapons and International Law* (New York, 1959), pp. 155-162, which leads to the same conclusion. For an authoritative discussion of radiation injuries see U. S. Armed Forces Special Weapons Project, *The Effects of Nuclear Weapons* (Washington, D. C., 1957), chap. xi, hereafter cited as *Effects of Nuclear Weapons* (1957).

[59]Cf. *U. S. Law of Land Warfare* (1956), Art. 37(b); *British Laws of War* (1958), Art. 112.

[60]Cf. *Effects of Nuclear Weapons* (1957), p. 428.

right to resort to gases, chemicals and bacteriological warfare.[61] It is generally accepted, however, that the prohibitions of the Geneva Gas Protocol, one agreement in a succession of conventions outlawing deleterious gases, today are declaratory of international customary law and thus binding on all states.[62] This, then, is another link in the chain of legal provisions which seems to spell the illegality of nuclear warfare even if directed against undoubted military objectives. If we add the long-range somatic and genetic effects which these weapons produce in their victims, it may also be considered within the orbit of biological warfare "which has been condemned by the conscience of mankind"[63] no less emphatically than poison gas and chemical warfare. . . .

The Dictates of Conscience

Granting that most of the international law of war lies in shambles and the "dictates of the public conscience" have seemingly surrendered to military expediency, in his dilemma the individual will find little guidance on the level of legality. Even if he could be sure—which he cannot be—that after a nuclear war nobody will be in a position to institute war crimes proceedings against anyone, he may still be troubled by the moral question. The incertitude of the collective conscience will force him back on his own personal judgment and sense of right.

It may well be, of course, that the dilemma "to press or not to press the button" will not be felt by very many. Indeed, one of the most distressing results of the degeneration of warfare in World War II has been the loss of appreciation, on the part of many otherwise honorable people, of the distinction between right and wrong in matters of warfare.[64] Aerial warfare and, *a fortiori*, long

[61]*U. S. Law of Land Warfare* (1956), Art. 38.

[62]Oppenheim-Lauterpacht, II (7th ed., 1952), 344; Stone, *op. cit.,* p. 556. F. D. Roosevelt, speaking of "poisonous or noxious gases or other inhumane devices of warfare," stated in 1943 that "the use of such weapons has been outlawed by the general opinion of civilized mankind" and that the United States would never resort to these weapons unless in retaliation for prior use by the enemy; quoted in Alexander N. Sack, "ABC—Atomic, Biological, Chemical Warfare in International Law," *Lawyers' Guild Review,* Vol. 10 (1950), p. 167. This statement raises the interesting but unanswerable question whether F. D. R. would have authorized the use of the atomic bomb on two densely populated Japanese cities. He had ordered its development to forestall a German effort and might have kept it in reserve, as gas was. Cf. J. M. Spaight, *The Atomic Problem* (London, 1948), p. 41.

[63]Oppenheim-Lauterpacht, II (7th ed., 1952), p. 348. See also Spaight, *Atomic Problem*, pp. 23-25; Greenspan, *op. cit.,* pp. 374-375.

[64]Cf. Sack, *Lawyers' Guild Review*, Vol. 5, p. 168.

distance missiles, have depersonalized the activity of killing and maiming. "Weapons with which the enemy can be attacked while he is at a distance," Clausewitz wrote in his treatise *On War*, "allow the feelings, the 'instinct for fighting' properly called, to remain almost at rest, and this so much the more according as the range of their effects is greater. With a sling we can imagine to ourselves a certain degree of anger accompanying the throw, there is less of this feeling in discharging a musket, and still less in firing a cannon shot,"[65] Today the distance between the soldier and the horror perpetrated on his victims is even greater and the amount of feeling accompanying the infliction of death and injury correspondingly smaller. In previous ages, notes a German atomic scientist, war was dreadful because man could become a wild animal. Today's wars are dreadful because man can exterminate his fellows as easily as vermin. "Not anger but the lack of feeling is our problem."[66] The depersonalization of the destructive process, warns Stone, "may yet render the principle of humanity as archaic as the principle of chivalry may already have become."[67]

This condition of declining moral sensitivity is all the more striking in view of the impressive regard paid today to the alleviation of suffering in our domestic life, in the treatment of the sick, the poor, criminals and even animals. Here the abhorrence of cruelty and respect for the sanctity of life have increased, while the clash of ideologies in the context of revolutionary developments in the art of killing has all but done away with any sense of common humanity in relation to the "enemy." That even the enemy is composed of human beings—men, women, and children—seems to have been forgotten; today, as C. Wright Mills notes correctly, "if men are acting in the name of 'their nation' they do not know moral limits but only expedient calculations."[68] Leading statesmen have agreed that war no longer is an acceptable "instrument of policy" in the adjustment of differences between nations, that it threatens to become a horror of slaughter and destruction intolerable to any decent mind. Yet public opinion accepts the need to use the weapons of annihilation. Secretary Forrestal, during the crisis created by the Berlin blockade in 1948, was worried whether the American public, should the need arise, would permit resort to the atomic bomb. It was the unanimous agreement of a score of

[65]Quoted in John U. Nef, *War and Human Progress: An Essay on the Rise of Industrial Civilization* (Cambridge, Mass., 1950), p. 372.

[66]Carl Friedrich von Weizsäcker, "Ethische and politische Probleme des Atomzeitalters," *Aussenpolitik*, Vol. 9 (1958), p. 305.

[67]Stone, *op. cit.*, p. 339.

[68]*The Causes of World War Three* (New York, 1958), pp. 79-80.

prominent newspaper publishers and editors, questioned by Forrestal, "that in the event of war the American people would not only have no question as to the propriety of the use of the atomic bomb but would in fact expect it to be used."[69] This acceptance of savagery as unavoidable is probably unchanged today. The equanimity with which in discussions of nuclear attacks entire metropolitan areas, if not countries, are written off is symptomatic of the same moral insensibility, of the turning of horror into morally condoned conventions of thinking.

And yet, there may be men for whom the moral dilemma will be real, who will not be content with doing their duty and imputing moral responsibility for their actions to their superiors. There may be men who, if and when faced with the consequences of the deeds they are asked to commit in the name of their nation, will want to follow the counsel of Thoreau to "be men first, and subjects afterwards."[70] Given the possibility that blind obedience to orders may lead not only to the killing of millions on the side of the enemy but may also spell the doom of one's own nation, and perhaps of mankind as such, a case could be made for the choice of disobedience even on grounds of prudence. Such loyalty to humanity might turn out to be the only meaningful national allegiance while at the same time preserving the moral integrity of the individual.

It is simple enough to point out that blind obedience is a relic of primitive man, that soldiers do not cease to be human beings, and that the best soldier is not necessarily the one who fights like a machine, regardless of the means and unaware of the moral meaning of victory. It is also true that no army could exist or operate if every man's personal standards of duty and morality were to prevail. The Nuremberg war criminal Jodl was right in saying "that the prosecution could thank its own obedient soldiers for being in a position to prosecute."[71] At the same time, one can find a powerful justification of the criticism of military policies on ethical grounds in the proved fallibility of the calculations of competent soldiers and statesmen. The decision to use the atomic bomb against Japan, for example, judged by the knowledge we have today of Japan's military

---

[69]Walter Millis (ed.), *The Forrestal Diaries* (New York, 1951), p. 487, quoted in Millis, *Arms and Men: A Study in American Military History* (New York, 1958), p. 289. By 1951, Millis adds, the American public "would probably have had little hesitation in incinerating any number of Communist troops—or Communist women and babies—in the nuclear fires" (p. 299).

[70]Henry David Thoreau, "Civil Disobedience," *Walden and Other Writings* (New York, 1950) p. 637.

[71]Related by Gilbert, *op. cit.*, p. 365.

potential in the summer of 1945, was probably a mistake. But even if the employment of the bomb spared the Allies an invasion and a bloody campaign in the main islands of Japan, a country claiming to defend the cause of freedom and the ultimate dignity of the individual human being cannot justify such a step on grounds of military strategy only. One cannot accept the argument that the shortening of a war is the supreme end without at the same time abandoning all moral restraints on the conduct of hostilities. This line of reasoning would justify not only the use of nuclear weapons but also the resort to poison gas, the dissemination of deadly germs, the torturing of prisoners, and mass killings of innocents by any other conceivable invention as long as strategists suppose they will be able to avoid the enemy's retaliation in kind. It may well be that the floodgates are already open to any atrocity that proves militarily effective. Yet who will be morally obtuse enough to deny the protest of an individual who refuses to be a party to what seems to him barbarism? Can one easily reject the eloquent plea of Sir Hartley Shawcross at the Nuremberg trials that "there comes a point where a man must refuse to answer to his leader, if he is also to answer to his conscience?"[72]

A number of religious leaders, men of diverse faiths, have argued that all-out nuclear war is not only suicidal as well as self-destructive in the sense of undermining the values we are seeking to preserve, but that it also violates absolute moral imperatives and therefore is morally wrong even if we could protect ourselves against nuclear attack. Speaking to the World Medical Congress in 1954, Pope Pius XII declared that the employment of ABC weapons, escaping from the control of man, is to be rejected as immoral: "Here it is no longer a question of defense against injustice and of the necessary safeguard of legitimate possessions, but of the annihilation, pure and simple of all human beings within its radius of action. This is not permitted on any account."[73] A committee set up by the World Council of Churches has concluded similarly that a military strategy contemplating the use of hydrogen bombs against urban centers violates "every element of Christian faith, hope and ethics." Christians should openly declare that such weapons should never be resorted to, and "if all out war should

---

[72]*Trial of the Major War Criminals before the International Military Tribunal*, Nuremberg 14 November 1945–1 October 1946, vol. III (Nuremberg, 1948), p. 144.

[73]Quoted in John Courtney Murray, S. J., "Remarks on the Moral Problem of War," *Theological Studies*, Vol. 20 (1959), p. 51.

occur, Christians should urge a cease fire, if necessary on the enemy's terms, and resort to non-violent resistance."[74] Others have counselled against retaliation with nuclear weapons against nuclear aggression on the ground that a nuclear war of defense today is a contradiction in terms. "The truth is that this would double the enormous evil physically and morally."[75] According to George F. Kennan, "the weapon of indiscriminate mass destruction goes farther than anything the Christian ethic can properly accept."[76]

It is clear that any unilateral renunciation of strategic nuclear weapons destroys the efficacy of the policy of deterrence and does away with the so-called "balance of terror." If one declares openly and in advance that these weapons will never be used, there is no conceivable reason for stockpiling them. The other side, then, could act as it saw fit and this might well lead to "nuclear blackmail" and ultimately defeat. Even merely to argue that, once the deterrent has failed to preserve peace, surrender is better than all-out nuclear war, weakens the effect of the deterrent, the strength of which depends on one's resolution to use it in retaliation. Yet it is probably true, as von Weizsacker puts it, that "these bombs can protect peace and freedom only on condition that they never fall, for if they should ever fall there would remain nothing worth protecting."[77] If so, the balance of terror amounts to a gigantic game of bluff, each side threatening the other side with weapons the use of which could not serve any sane purpose. Unless the absurd immorality of a world nuclear conflict is kept in mind and reaffirmed constantly, nations may lose the sense of restraint which today still makes nuclear arsenals a deterrent threat rather than weapons readily used. That such moral affirmations may weaken the restraints upon would-be aggressors and, therefore, encourage aggression, tyranny and immorality is

[74]World Council of Churches, Division of Studies, *Christians and the Prevention of War in an Atomic Age—A Theological Discussion* (n.p., 1958), p. 30.

[75]Francis P. Stratmann, O.P., *War and Christianity Today*, trans. John Doebele (London, 1956), p. 57. That retaliation will not serve any positive end is fairly clear. "Rationally, of course," writes John H. Herz in his excellent study *International Politics in the Atomic Age* (New York, 1959), p. 189, "there is no 'reason' for the attacked, once his threat of retaliation has proved futile, actually to make good on his threat and retaliate; he will do so only to satisfy his 'irrational' urge for revenge." Instead of achieving the prevention of a take-over by the enemy, retaliation may well lead to counter-retaliation or even a series of desperate nuclear exchanges, which eventually may threaten human life everywhere.

[76]"Foreign Policy and Christian Conscience," *Atlantic Monthly*, May 1959, p. 47.

[77]*Aussenpolitik*, IX, 306.

another of the paradoxes inherent in the situation of mutual deterrence.

The subordinate in front of the button may have neither time nor inclination to think of all these complexities. Yet these considerations must not be ignored. The remarks of Karl Jaspers, speaking of the declaration made in 1957 by eighteen outstanding German physicists not to participate in the making of atomic weapons, are pertinent: "The personal 'No' is unassailable as long as it represents an act of conscience and therefore becomes a visible event only when others bring it before the public. It is unassailable only then when one also accepts personal responsibility for all consequences."[78] Whether all possible consequences of pressing or not pressing the button can be foreseen is doubtful. It is obvious that an individual can not restrict the effects of such a choice to his own personal life. The conscientious objector in wars past could remain faithful to the dictates of his conscience without thereby significantly influencing the outcome of the armed conflict. Today, given the potency of the new weapons, the refusal to obey on the part of a single important individual could spell a nation's defeat, though it might save the world from ruin, and so would make his decision all the more fateful. He would have to weigh the claims of the present generation against those of the future, the possibility of the adversary's world triumph against the danger of race suicide. He would have to answer the question whether any single individual should make the fateful choice for all humanity. And he might wonder what could be the justification of choosing non-existence for those who, in the years ahead, would have been born into life.

[78]*Die Atombombe und die Zukunft des Menschens: Politisches Bewusstsein in unserer Zeit* (3d. ed.; Munich, 1958), p. 274.

Selected Bibliography

Allen, J. L. "The Relation of Strategy and Morality," *Ethics*, Vol. 73 (1963), p. 167.

Avineri, S. "The Problem of War in Hegel's Thought," *Journal of the History of Ideas*, Vol. 22 (1960), p. 463.

Bennett, John C. (ed.). *Nuclear Weapons and the Conflict of Conscience.* New York: Charles Scribner's, 1962.

Bramson, Leon, and Goethals, George (eds). *War: Studies from Psychology, Sociology, Anthropology.* New York: Basic Books, 1964.

Buchan, Alastan. *War in Modern Society.* London: C. A. Watts and Co. Ltd., 1966.

Clausewitz, Karl von, *On War,* new and revised ed. London: Routledge, 1962.

Falk, Richard A. *Law, Morality, and War in the Contemporary World.* New York: Frederick A. Praeger, 1963.

Hartigan, R. S. "Noncombatant Immunity: Reflections on Its Origins and Present Status," *Review of Politics,* Vol. 29 (1967), p. 204.

―――― "Saint Augustine on War and Killing: The Problem of the Innocent," *Journal of the History of Ideas,* Vol. 27 (1966), p. 195.

Irmscher, William F. (ed.). *Man and Warfare.* Boston: Little, Brown and Co., 1964.

Kotzsch, Lothar. *The Concept of War in Contemporary History and International Law.* Geneva: Librairie E. Droz, 1956.

Krickers, R. J. "On the Morality of Chemical/Biological Warfare," *Journal of Conflict Resolution,* Vol. 9 (1965), p. 200.

Lynd, Staughton (ed.). *Nonviolence in America: A Documentary History.* Indianapolis: Bobbs-Merrill Co., 1966.

Mayer, Peter (ed.). *The Pacifist Conscience.* Chicago: Henry Regnery Co., 1966.

McKenna, J. C. "Ethics and War: A Catholic View," *American Political Science Review*, Vol. 54 (1960), p. 647.

Miller, L. H. "Contemporary Significance of the Doctrine of Just War," *World Politics*, Vol. 16 (1964), p. 254.

Nagle, William J. (ed.). *Morality and Modern Warfare*. Baltimore: Helicon Press, 1960.

Narveson, Jan. "Pacifism: A Philosophical Analysis—A Rejoinder," *Ethics*, Vol. 78 (1964-65), p. 148.

Palter, R. M. "The Ethics of Extermination," *Ethics*, Vol. 74 (1964), p. 208.

Ramsey, Paul. "Ethics of Intervention," *Review of Politics*, Vol. 27 (1965), p. 287.

——. *War and the Christian Conscience*. Durham, N.C.: Duke University Press, 1961.

Russell, Bertrand. *Which Way to Peace?* London: M. Joseph, 1937.

——. *Why Men Fight*. New York: Century, 1917.

Sibley, Mulford Q. (ed.). *The Quiet Battle*. Boston: Beacon Press, 1963.

Smith, C. I. "Hegel on War," *Journal of the History of Ideas*, Vol. 26 (1965), p. 282.

Stein, Walter (ed.). *Nuclear Weapons: A Catholic Response*. New York: Sheed and Ward, 1961.

Strachey, Alex. *The Unconscious Motives of War: A Psychoanalytic Contribution*. New York: International University Press, 1957.

Tucker, Robert W. *The Just War*. Baltimore: The Johns Hopkins Press, 1960.

——. "Peace and War," *World Politics*, Vol. 17 (1965), p. 310.

Waltz, K. N. "Kant, Liberalism and War," *American Political Science Review*, Vol. 56 (1962), p. 331.

Walzer, Michael. "Exodus 32 and the Theory of Holy War: The History of a Citation," *Harvard Theological Review*, Vol. 61 (1968), p. 1.

Weinberg, Arthur and Lila (eds.). *Instead of Violence*. Boston: Beacon Press, 1963.

Wells, Donald A. *The War Myth*. New York: Pegasus, 1967.

Whitman, M. J. "Pacifism: A Philosophical Analysis—A Reply," *Ethics*, Vol. 76 (1966), p. 307.

Wright, Quincy. *A Study of War*. Chicago: University of Chicago Press, 1942.

Zahn, Gordon C. *War, Conscience, and Dissent*. New York: Hawthorne Books, Inc., 1967.